Paul Preuss, Lord of the Abyss

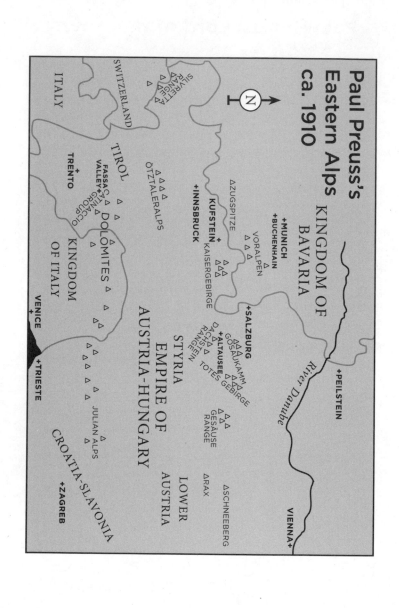

PAUL PREUSS
Lord of the Abyss

Life and Death
at the Birth of Free-Climbing

By David Smart

RMB

For information on purchasing bulk quantities of this book, or to
obtain media excerpts or invite the author to speak at an event,
please visit rmbooks.com and select the "Contact" tab.

RMB | Rocky Mountain Books Ltd.
rmbooks.com
@rmbooks
facebook.com/rmbooks

Cataloguing data available from Library and Archives Canada
ISBN 9781771603232 (hardcover)
ISBN 9781771603249 (electronic)

Printed and bound in Canada

We would like to also take this opportunity to acknowledge the traditional
territories upon which we live and work. In Calgary, Alberta, we acknowledge
the Niitsitapi (Blackfoot) and the people of the Treaty 7 region in Southern
Alberta, which includes the Siksika, the Piikuni, the Kainai, the Tsuut'ina and
the Stoney Nakoda First Nations, including Chiniki, Bearpaw, and Wesley First
Nations. The City of Calgary is also home to Métis Nation of Alberta, Region
III. In Victoria, British Columbia, we acknowledge the traditional territories
of the Lkwungen (Esquimalt, and Songhees), Malahat, Pacheedaht, Scia'new,
T'Sou-ke and W̱SÁNEĆ (Pauquachin, Tsartlip, Tsawout, Tseycum) peoples.

We acknowledge the financial support of the Government of Canada
through the Canada Book Fund and the Canada Council for the
Arts, and of the province of British Columbia through the British
Columbia Arts Council and the Book Publishing Tax Credit.

Paolo Preuss was Lord of the Abyss.
—Giovanni Battista "Tita" Piaz

For Katrina.

Contents

Introduction: Paul Preuss, Legend

But because of this very troublesomeness and
Indigestibility he was, in the midst of such a limpid
and prearranged little world, a constant source
of vital unrest, a reproach, an admonition and
warning, a spur to new, bold, forbidden, intrepid
ideas, an unruly, stubborn sheep in the herd.

—Hermann Hesse, *The Glass Bead Game.*

Many modern climbers have never heard of Paul Preuss. Few English-speaking climbers are sure how to pronounce his name ("Proyce"). This was not always the case. George Mallory, who died on Mount Everest in 1924, and uttered that he had attempted it "because it is there," also said "no one will ever equal Preuss." Hans Dülfer, the top rock climber in the Eastern Alps in Preuss's time, had roped up with Preuss and called him "the complete master." Tita Piaz, the so-called Devil of the Dolomites, dubbed Preuss "the most fantastic knight of the mountains of all times and all nations." His friends considered him "an almost supernatural being, born for the rock." Eugen Lammer, Viennese mountaineering writer and top climber in his time, said "his daily bread was the highest ethics of alpinism." The best Italian rock climber of the 1930s, Emilio Comici, said he was "the dominator of the mountain, the unsurpassable master of pure climbing." Willo Welzenbach, the inventor of the first climbing grade system and great climber of the 1930s said "Preuss's climbing was incomparable, unique." Austrian and fellow Viennese Fritz Kasparek, a member of the team that made the first ascent of the Eigerwand, said "Paul Preuss was the ideal alpinist." Giusto Gervasutti, the Italian who made numerous hard first ascents in the Alps in the 1940s, was known superlatively as "Il Fortissimo" ("The Hardest") but acknowledged Preuss as "unsurpassed and unsurpassable." Paul Preuss so impressed Reinhold Messner, the great Italian mountaineer who soloed Mount Everest without oxygen in 1980, and the first climber to ascend all 14 8000-metre peaks, that he built a mountaineering museum around Preuss's piton hammer, wrote two books about him and instituted a foundation in Preuss's name.

In the months before his death, Preuss's presentations on his climbing adventures drew crowds from beyond the climbing community and filled concert halls in Austria, Italy and Germany. Yet, when he died at 27, climbing without pitons or even a belay, he had no clear successor to his ideals. Without him, climbing may never have developed the ethical, existential core that gave it meaning in the long term. But even the most trenchant traditionalists remain unsure about whether to add him to their pantheon or dismiss him as at worst a lunatic or, at best, an indelicate subject best ignored.

Why is Preuss such a controversial figure? Why did he care so much about climbing ethics? What set him on his dangerous career as a free-soloist and a legend? What does the legend mean, if anything, for climbing today?

The Boy Who Loved Flowers and Mountains

*....to childhood illness that so strangely began
with a number of profound and grave transform-
ations, to days in rooms withdrawn and quiet...*

—Rainer Maria Rilke,
The Notebooks of Malte Laurids Brigge

I t was a beautiful summer day in the Dolomites, and the pale
yellow, square-sided plinth of the Campanile Basso lay against
blue skies. The Campanile was an expert's climb, even by its Via
Normale, but on this rare day, a party of three had undertaken it.
They had stopped for a break on the long ledge called the Via Stadone, 150 metres below the flat summit.

As often happened in the history of climbing, the seemingly
peaceful weather had set the stage for a dangerous and unprecedented event. While two of the climbers waited, a third, Paul
Preuss, went on alone onto the East Face, a wall that had been declared impossible by the best climbers in the world.

Expert climbers were associated with intense masculinity –
hoary moustaches and grim expressions – but this soloist was a
small, blond-haired, blue-eyed young man in a purple silk necktie,
green lederhosen and a well-cut Janker jacket. He sang obscene
Viennese street songs to himself and giggled as he climbed. The
young woman on the ledge below, his sister Mina, asked him what
he could see. Not much, he joked, and climbed on up the impossible East Face.

The climb was so outrageous in concept that he had kept his plans
secret from Mina and the third member of their party, his college
friend and favourite climbing partner, Paul Relly. Relly snapped
a picture of Preuss before he climbed out of sight, no doubt wondering if it would be the last ever taken of his friend alive. Why

was Preuss doing this? Just a week before, he had soloed the West Face of the Totenkirchl, one of the hardest rock climbs in the Alps. What did he have left to prove? Yet Paul Preuss had never been one to measure himself against other climbers.

Together with Preuss, Relly had made his way through the heady days of undergraduate life, climbing-club meetings, romances and drinking sessions. Handsome, rich, educated and talented, Relly shared with Preuss a single liability: they were both Jewish, by race if not by religious faith. Relly had fallen in love with the Preuss family's way of life. They had assimilated not to the sterile parlour-life of Vienna but to the Styrian mountains that Relly loved. The family's progeny astounded Relly: his friend, now slaying one of the greatest problems of the Alps alone; and, beside him on the ledge, beautiful, dark-haired, lithe Mina, with whom Relly was deeply in love. Looking into her eyes now, at the apex of his love for the Preusses, Relly realized that Mina felt the same way towards him.

When Preuss reached the summit, he signed the register and then took a moment to consider his options. The route had been difficult, but whether the adventure had ended too soon, or had just been a little easier than expected, he decided to downclimb the Via Normale.

Reunited with Mina and Relly, he learned that they were engaged to be married. The Campanile; a new brother, and not just of the rope; one of his two sisters well married. It had been a remarkable day, and it was not even over. He led them up the Via Normale to make his third trip on the Campanile in a single day.

Paul Preuss's extraordinary life was, more than most, the result of choices made by his two extraordinary parents, Eduard Preuss and Lina Lauchheim. Paul's religious experience, love of mountains and nature, drive to succeed and also to assimilate, cosmopolitan outlook and facility with languages all bore the imprint of his parents' aspirations and struggles.

In 1867, Eduard Preuss, Paul's future father, was 18 years old. Whenever he could, he wandered the hilly Mecsek forests near his home in Pécs, in the Hungarian province of Baranya. He was an amateur botanist and searched the cracks of the limestone out-crops in the shadows of hilltop castles and the remains of Roman forts for rare hellebores and ophyrs. In late afternoon, when the shadows of the ancient oaks darkened the forest floor, he left the solitude of nature and made his way back to town, a patchwork of medieval buildings that straddled the dark, slow waters of the Danube.

Eduard's other love was music. On the way home, he visited the organ maker's workshop to watch and listen as the craftsmen tapped the tuning collar of a flue pipe. A crucifix on the workshop wall, however, reminded him that the church instruments made here would not be played by Jews like him. Next to the cross hung the more hopeful image of the emperor. In 1867, Franz Joseph I had ascended to the throne of the empire of Austria-Hungary. Al-though an absolutist who relished his 30-odd regal titles, which included impressive-sounding archaisms like Grand Voivode of the Voivodeship of Serbia, Franz Joseph fancied himself a liberal when it came to religious freedom. One of his first acts as ruler had been to open academic and judicial professions to his Jewish subjects.

Although Eduard would never play an organ in church, he had found a musical outlet in the piano, an instrument that knew no religious creed. He was already skilled enough to give lessons, and for the rest of his life, he described his profession as "pianist." Since most well-to-do households possessed both children and pianos, and Franz Joseph had removed barriers to the employ-ment of Jews like him, Eduard saw a path to a career.

Preuss was both an old Ashkenazi Jewish word for a Prussian and a common gentile surname. The Preusses might have des-cended from the German families brought to Southern Hungary to repopulate it after the Hapsburgs drove out the Ottomans in 1699. The name may have also been taken as recently as 1793, when new laws required Jewish families who had not used last names to adopt them for tax purposes.

The empire was a patchwork of German, Hungarian, Polish, Ladin, Czech, Ukrainian, Slovak, Slovene, Croatian, Serb, Italian and Romanian ethnic groups practising many types of Judaism,

Christianity and Islam. Ethnic groups, especially Jews, were targets of intolerance and, occasionally, violence. Many Jews, like Eduard, chose to reduce the chances of persecution by assimilating into the Austrian gentile majority, assuming their dress and behaviour. Assimilation, however, was a double-edged sword: it would never satisfy anti-Semites, who could still passively act upon or openly express their prejudices.

For most of Eduard's life, the greatest threat to peace came from neighbour states, but ethnic strife simmered within Austria-Hungary's borders too. In 1849, the year of Eduard's birth, Croatian and Hungarian nationalists had fought the Austrian army for the possession of Pécs. Austria-Hungary was a state of anomalies and contradictions. Most visitors in the late 19th and early 20th centuries either ignored or avoided ethnic stress and war, and reported a land of civility, culture and beauty.

Without crossing an international border, a traveller could visit the vast Eurasian Steppe, hunt boar in the oldest forests in Europe, climb the glaciated high peaks of the Alps and look down into Switzerland, stay in Italian towns in the Dolomites and wade into the Mediterranean from palm-lined beaches. The empire also boasted some of the oldest and finest cities in Europe. Prague, Budapest and Vienna had ancient universities, modern industries and institutions that nurtured art, music, dance and architecture.

Poverty, disease and political turmoil also thrived in the imperial cities, and nowhere more so than in the imperial capital. Vienna, some 275 kilometres to the north of Pécs, had become one of the largest, most cosmopolitan cities in Europe. Between 1880 and 1890, it doubled its population from three-quarters of a million to a million-and-a-half inhabitants. Its citizens hailed from everywhere in the empire and beyond; 140,000 Jews called it home.

Many Jews found the capital's promise of diversity and social mobility irresistible. In 1867, Eduard's next-oldest brother, Sigmund, took advantage of the new liberal mood and enrolled in law school at the University of Vienna. Eduard applied to the Vienna Conservatory to train as a piano instructor. The other Preuss brothers, Colomon and Adolf, later followed Sigmund and Eduard to the city, but the two original Preuss pioneers from Baranya remained closer to each other than anyone else in their family. Throughout their lives, they shared flats, vacationed together and looked out for each other.

The Vienna Conservatory accepted only the finest students. Its first director had been the maestro Antonio Salieri, who had taught Franz Liszt, Franz Schubert and Ludwig van Beethoven. Eduard was talented and passed the rigorous entrance auditions under the scrutiny of the director of music, Anton Rubinstein, one of the best pianists of the 19th century. In 1872, Johannes Brahms won the directorship, partly on the strength of the critical acclaim for his recent *A German Requiem*, op. 45, and string compositions. Brahms was almost twice Eduard's age, but he and Eduard became fast friends.

In Vienna, butchers had been made lords, paupers had become tycoons, penniless artists had become royal favourites. Likewise, the Preuss brothers rose from their humble background to become men of substance. Eduard, the provincial Jewish boy who used to watch the town craftsmen build church organs, now consorted with the world's greatest musical minds; Sigmund, although a Hungarian Jew, prepared to take his Austrian judge's examinations.

When Eduard graduated, he became a professor of the keyboard at the conservatory. Eduard's talent as a concert pianist and instructor caught the attention of the aristocratic benefactors in the Society of Friends of Music in Vienna. Soon, he had a part-time job as a piano teacher of the children of some of Austria's most powerful families.

Eduard indulged his love of nature in the nearby Vienna Woods – the Rax, Schneeberg and Hohe Wand, collectively known as the Hausbergen. There, hikers, skiers and climbers could patronize bars, restaurants, hotels and huts with accommodations that ranged from the economy *Matratzenlager* to private rooms. Mapped and marked hiking trails of all difficulties criss-crossed the forests and mountains. Those in search of sport could bag the summit of the Schneeberg, schuss down groomed ski runs in a dozen areas (and walk back to the top, as the ski lift had not yet been invented) or tackle the popular technical rock climbs at the numerous *Klettergärten* (the German plural of *Klettergarten*, or climbing garden).

Weekend forays in the Hausbergen inspired Eduard to explore the higher Austrian Alps to the west. The rocky Gesäuse range, the Dachstein Mountains, the Ötztal Mountains and the Silvretta range on the border with Switzerland promised adventure, natural beauty and charming rustic culture. Getting to the mountains before the advent of paved public highways and automobiles, however, remained a challenge for Eduard and other Viennese *Bergfreunde* – mountain enthusiasts without aspirations to technical climbing.

The emperor came to their aid. In 1877, by Franz Joseph's edict, the Imperial Royal Austrian State Railways opened a line through the Salzkammergut in Styria. The region, named for the salt mines first excavated by the Romans, offered the beauty of the Alps and the charm of the rustic traditions of the local farmers and woodsmen, known as *Senners*.

The railway stopped at the aristocratic summer retreat of Altmünster am Traunsee and also reached picturesque, remote villages such as Altaussee, next to the Aussee, whose waters reflected the desolate walls of the Totes Gebirge (Dead Mountains). The *Senners* preserved their traditional appearance and customs: men laboured in the fields and pastures in their green Ausseer *Tracht*, and women went about their work in the Ausseer dirndl with lavender-dyed skirts. Locals still observed medieval mummer's ceremonies like *Glöckler und Berigeln* that had disappeared elsewhere.

In one sense, however, the people of Altaussee were more modern than those of other valleys: with some painful exceptions, they welcomed Jewish vacationers. Zionist writer Theodor Herzl and psychoanalyst Sigmund Freud were among the region's Jewish visitors.

Eduard had first heard of the area from Brahms, who had rented a summer house there since the 1860s. The Preuss brothers had lived in Vienna ten years, and they now earned respectable wages. In 1877, they took advantage of the modern novelty of the

Salzkammergut railway to make their first summer vacation to the mountains of Styria.

Caroline Lauchheim, who would one day become Paul's mother, was 13 years old in August 1870, when the Prussian army surrounded her hometown of Strasbourg. The beautiful medieval city was the capital of the ethnically Franco-German French region of Alsace, and according to the Prussian chancellor, Otto von Bismarck, rightfully part of Germany. After a few days, when the city still had not surrendered, the Prussians indiscriminately bombarded it with artillery.

A young Alsatian woman trapped in the city described the siege in her diary:

> The regular bombardment of the town has begun! The threat of our foes is being carried out, and, after a consecutive fire which lasted thirteen hours, we understand its fateful meaning. A rain of projectiles of all sizes fell upon ever quarter of our town. Several public buildings are actually destroyed, others are greatly damaged; not even the hospital, with its sick and wounded has been spared... several have been killed in their beds. A great many of the inhabitants of our Faubourgs are crowding the streets of the inner town, wandering around in search of shelter. The misery of the poor is also very great, and the price of food is rising daily. But all are ready to endure with patience any kind of privation, to undergo any trial, and all classes of people show a heroism which is surprising.[1]

Caroline – or Lina, as she was known to her family – volunteered to fold bandages for the wounded at the Red Cross hospital set up in the seminary by Saint Thomas's Church.[2] Despite the bravery and endurance of the population, however, the ruined city fell to the invaders on September 28, after six weeks of bombardment. The German army held a victory service in Saint Thomas's.

The war ended in the spring of 1871, and the French ceded Alsace to the Germans. The Lauchheims could neither live under

German occupation nor forgive the French, who had surrendered their homeland to the invaders. They moved instead to Vienna, famous for welcoming, or at least accepting, Europe's refugees. Although by nature tactful and well mannered, Lina remained bitter about the war for the rest of her life and occasionally scandalized polite company by using the anti-German epithet *boche*.

In 1876, Lina completed the six years of public education Austria provided for girls. University, however, was out of the question. Even if her family had had the means, women would not be allowed to enrol in Austrian universities for another 15 years. The position of governess was one of the few options open to educated, intelligent, ambitious young women like Lina. Those qualities, as well as her facility in Italian, French and German, made Lina a natural candidate, and she secured a position with the family of Baron von Rosenberg as a tutor and governess to his two sons.

Governesses occupied a social niche above the regular household employees. They had to have the right bearing, intelligence and accent. Young women who could speak French were considered especially suitable, but other foreigners were also desirable because the governess prepared boys for entry into a transnational aristocratic world. A governess had to be strong and self-assured. Although respected by the family, she ate and lived with the servants, who often resented her superior position.

Every year, from May to October, the Rosenbergs and their staff decamped to the alpine setting of Altmünster am Traunsee to summer in the baroque splendour of Schloss Ebenzweier. For Lina, however, gilded ballrooms could not compete with the views of the Traunsee, the wooded hillsides and the mountains. She often hiked up the Gmundnerberg above the town to admire the view of the lake and the Traunstein, the steep-sided rock peak on the eastern shore over which the sun rose each morning.

She found a guide to take her and the Rosenberg boys across the lake to attempt the long and strenuous hike up the 1700-metre-high Traunstein. When the boys became too tired to continue, she left them with the guide and made for the top alone. On the summit, she was rewarded with a panorama of the Dachstein range, the Totes Gebirge and the crocodile's-back ridge of the Gosau in the distance.

The mountains had a timeless beauty, but Lina's future became less certain as the boys grew. When they went off to school, Lina would need to find a new position or marry out of the service. It was very difficult to meet eligible bachelors as a governess. The senior servants were all too old, and the junior servants were below her in status and lacked her education. Marrying into her employer's family was frowned upon, and few eligible bachelors were willing to marry mere governesses. But Lina had faith in herself and had never taken a passive role in her life. She had aided the wounded during the fight to keep the Prussians out of Strasbourg and, when that battle was lost, built a new life in faraway Vienna. Lina Lauchheim was a young woman who took control of her own life. Her eyes were open for opportunities.

In the late 1870s, Eduard Preuss spent his summers in Altaussee. He rented rooms from *Senners* who welcomed tourists into their homes in the summer to make a little extra money. The mountains, the lake, the pastoral setting and the friendly *Senners* had made Altaussee popular with artists, intellectuals and *Bergfreunde*. Despite Eduard's cosmopolitan background, he had come from a small town and loved the people, the woods and the mountains. His growing body of knowledge of local history, geology, folklore and flora helped him to overcome the locals' xenophobia more quickly than tourists who only took an interest in the alpine landscape.

Like many bourgeois hobbyists of his day, Eduard sought out and joined a club where he could share and further his interests. He chose the Austrian Alpine Club, founded in 1862, when the only other alpine organization in the world was the Alpine Club, a coterie of elite British climbers based in London. Unlike their British counterpart, the Austrian Alpine Club and the German Alpine Club (established in 1869) were federations of smaller, independent sections with their own criteria for membership and their own mountain-based interests. The Austrian club had been founded by geologist-climbers and *Bergfreunde* to undertake scientific research in the alpine environment and to encourage safe, aesthetic enjoyment of the mountains. Technical climbing was the domain of a minority of its members. In 1873, the Austrian group merged with the German Alpine Club to form the German and Austrian Alpine Club, hereafter referred to as the Alpine Club. The new body had 400 sections, each with its own criteria for membership and was some 100,000 *Bergfreunde* strong, including the ten members of Eduard Preuss's Aussee Section.

The Alpine Club encouraged infrastructure building to make the mountains accessible to its preponderantly urban membership. Individual sections accrued impressive debts to pay for the actual trails and huts.[3] Joseph Lux, a pioneer of amateur photography, explained the aesthetic reasoning behind this program in the *German Alpine Times* in 1910: the "beauty of nature would stand lonely and unrecognized and wondered at by nobody if it wasn't for art,"[4] and art relied on trails and huts.

Trail designers strove for safe ways to enjoy the views. In its 1900 annual report, the Bayerland Section declared that it designed trails not to ameliorate risk but to eradicate it: "It seems to us to be an irrefutable necessity to fashion the access path to the hut in such a way so that it can be walked up without danger… Building a completely safe climb will also provide these visitors with the opportunity of insight into one of the most awesome rock sceneries…"[5]

The Aussee Section shared in this passion. In 1879, its activities included boat trips; hikes to passes, lakes or villages; and several communal meals – but not a single roped climb.[6] Members included well-educated doctors, lawyers and professors, who paid club dues not just to share their interests with like-minded individuals but for the privilege of doing so safely and comfortably. Sigmund Freud, like many aging mountain enthusiasts, valued this privilege so highly that he kept up his Alpine Club memberships long after he ceased climbing.[7]

Eduard was occasionally drawn to more adventurous peaks, like the Sarstein in the Dachstein Mountains. To have climbed harder, he would have needed a guide. In Austria, however, the demand for guides' services, and therefore their availability, was low. Tourists in need of guides preferred the higher Western Alps. In Austria, the guideless climbing philosophies of Ludwig Purtscheller, Eugen Lammer and Emil Zsigmondy were popular. A three-day mountain guide's course held in Austria in 1900 was sparsely attended. In 1908, the talented and energetic guide Konrad (changed to Conrad after he emigrated to Canada) Kain invented in English lessons in Vienna so that he could take a job in the Canadian Rockies rather than continue to eke out a living in the Austrian Alps.

In 1882, 33-year-old Eduard had a prestigious position at the conservatory, and a mountain hideaway where he could teach music to the children of vacationing nobility. In the city, his colleagues included some of the greatest musicians, artists and composers in the world. His friend Brahms still rented summer lodgings on the Aussee – as did composer Robert Schumann and his wife, Clara, a piano virtuoso rumoured to be Brahms's mistress. Only the possibility that Eduard would remain a bachelor compromised this picture of bourgeois success.

In July, Eduard's reputation as a piano teacher reached Baron von Rosenberg in Schloss Ebenzweier. The baron, who had an eye for talented help, asked Eduard if he might come to the castle twice a week to give his sons piano lessons. Eduard took the same railway that had brought him to Altaussee on his first excursion to the Salzkammergut. At the Altmünster am Traunsee station, a carriage awaited him. In the music room of the *Schloss*, their charming French tutor, 25-year-old Lina Lauchheim, introduced Eduard to the Baron's sons.

The two Rosenberg employees felt an immediate, mutual attraction, despite their differences. Lina was a refugee and a Protestant in a Catholic aristocratic setting, Eduard a shy Hungarian Jew who had sought his fortune in Vienna, but they shared a cultured, cosmopolitan outlook and a love of mountains. They courted over the summer, and on one occasion, Lina brought the baron's boys to visit Eduard in Aussee for the day.

On September 12, 1882, they married in Vienna. As a measure of how smitten Lina was, she converted to Judaism despite her Protestant piety, to placate the Preuss family and ensure that their children would be Jews, according to tradition.[8] They received a prescient wedding gift: a painting by Eduard's friend Baron de Ben. The artist had gone to some trouble to climb up a gully below the Gosau to paint a unique view of the Scharwand hut and the formidable rock walls of the Gosau, where Paul would later climb.

The newlyweds rented a two-bedroom apartment at number 39 on the Ringstrasse on the Franz Joseph Quay in Vienna. Sigmund, now a judge, rented the second bedroom. A year later, on July 30, 1883, their first child was born. They named her after the emperor's popular daughter, Archduchess Sophie. On October 30, 1884, at the end of the summer vacation in Altaussee, a second daughter was born – Wilhelmine, known throughout her life as Mina.

In 1886, Eduard purchased 53 Puchen Street, a handsome house built in the traditional Styrian style. There, at 1:30 in the morning on August 19, 1886, beneath de Ben's painting of the Gosau, Lina gave birth to a son. It was Emperor Franz Joseph's birthday, a holiday in Austria-Hungary. Flags and banners decorated the moonlit houses of the village. "In the moonlight," said Severino Casara, Paul's most adoring biographer, "the mountains outside are burning braziers, celebrating the birth of a new emperor, their own beloved son."[9]

They named the boy Paul, a name usually avoided by Jews because of its association with the fiery Christian evangelist and opponent of Judaism, Paul of Tarsus. Neither Paul's last nor his first name identified him as a Jew. He was born in the mountains, and already on the path of assimilation.

Photographers have shown how climbers' faces eventually become ciphers for the concentration and stresses of their vocation. Their appearance before they climbed – a narrowness in the eyes, the set of a mouth, the easy hang of their limbs, or some other sign – may likewise presage their destiny. An outdoor family portrait commemorated Paul's aunts' and uncles' visit to Altaussee in the summer of 1895. Sigmund, Coloman and Eduard wore dark city suits and hats. Eduard smiled contentedly beneath his moustache. Paul wore a young boy's sailor suit and hat. He was a slender, handsome boy with a high forehead and long cheekbones. His big eyes and frown made him look a little sad. The others all wore hats, but Paul's head of blond hair remained uncovered. He must have been proud of it: for the rest of his life, even in the high mountains, he rarely wore a hat.

Despite Paul's natural ability to make friends, his religion and bourgeois family impeded his integration into Catholic, rustic Altaussee. He had only a couple of playmates among the neighbourhood boys, notably the Mittler brothers, Franz and Otto. Like every local boy, he learned the local lore, the dialect and the names of the mountains and streams. Without many playmates, he spent countless hours with his sisters, with whom he remained close for the rest of his life.

Paul's parents cultivated a sense of bourgeois identity in their children. Eduard instructed the children on the piano, a symbol of urbane, cultured life. Sophie excelled, but Paul, although fond of loudly singing as he hiked, had little musical talent. His sisters dreaded rainy days stuck in the house while he practised.

Eduard accepted Paul's lack of musicianship and consoled himself with the boy's natural ability at chess, Eduard's favourite game. Lina spoke to the children in French. After his polyglot youth, Paul would find it easy to pick up other languages, such as English and Italian. He also inherited from his father a basic knowledge of the natural sciences; they took long walks together in the meadows and forests, and Paul learned the names of the plants and trees. He expressed his fascination with nature with unabashed sincerity. "Father," he said after one outdoor excursion, "I love mountains and flowers so much!"[10]

Love, to paraphrase Grimm, is a treasure found in a dark place; like death, it is something we all eventually find in our own way, and in our own time. It can be avoided but neither cheated nor put off forever. Love came early to Paul. The object of his love, the mountains, inspired joy and a kind of fairy-tale dread reflected in impressions he later recorded. There is a childlike awe in a description he wrote of the Trisselwand as an adult: although it had become an easy climb for him, it still exuded "eerie charm," and its face was a "gloomy wall which looks down above green forests to the lakeshore."[11]

His solitary habits in the mountains had a melancholy element. When Schumann, Brahms or some other colleague joined Eduard and Paul on a hike and the adults' conversation bored Paul, he wandered out of sight for hours on his own. Eduard eventually equipped Paul with a small steel signalling mirror and a tin whistle in case he got lost. The whistle remained silent in Paul's back pocket, a talisman of protection and an admission of vulnerability.

At the end of every alpine vacation season, Eduard and his family followed his aristocratic students back to Vienna, where he maintained his position at the conservatory. The Preusses' life at 39 Ringstrasse was deeply connected to the city's high culture, but a sinister, invisible threat was afoot. Viennese risked infection from a host of major and minor illnesses, especially in the winter months. No address was immune, and the field of antibiotics had progressed little, so residents simply went about their lives and hoped for the best.

One morning in the fall of 1894, as the family sat down to breakfast, Paul called out that he could not move his legs to get out of bed. The doctor could do little besides diagnose the source of Paul's paralysis: poliomyelitis, or polio – an inflammation of the grey matter of the spine that causes paralysis that can be permanent and impede the normal growth of the affected limbs in children. In rare cases, the infection can kill the host. Many victims recover completely, but many suffer from lifelong paralysis.

By 1894, researchers had discovered that the disease entered the body through the intestinal tract, usually from water infected with fecal matter. In 1908, Viennese doctor Karl Landsteiner identified the virus; his tests of the Viennese water system found so much poliomyelitis that he fled the city. Opportunities abounded to ingest the numerous viruses in the water. There was no polio vaccine until the 1950s, and today there is still no cure. Predictably, popular 19th-century treatments, such as nut-meal baths, poultices of exotic ingredients like chamomile, slippery elm, sweet almond oil, and spikenard oil had no effect on the paralysis in Paul's legs.

In June, after Paul's quarantine had been lifted, he still could not move his body below the waist. The family moved back to Altaussee for the summer; alpine air and high-altitude sunshine were still prescribed for afflictions ranging from tuberculosis to alcoholism. Paul's wicker wheelchair was parked in the sun on the lawn of 53 Puchen. For weeks, his condition did not change.

One morning, the housemaid found Paul's wheelchair empty and its occupant crawling across the lawn. The family was ecstatic. Eduard did not intend to wait for nature to take its own course of recovery. He held Paul under the arms while he took his first steps and began a program of leg raises, lunges, arm swings and other physical drills popular with 19th-century "physical culture" enthusiasts. After a few weeks, Paul walked unassisted.

Eduard and Paul returned to the mountains. Their hikes started out at about eight kilometres and gradually became longer and harder, as if Eduard needed more and more dramatic proof that his son was on the road to recovery. Endurance ran in the family. Paul's 80-year-old grandmother tagged along on a 20-kilometre hike. She had come all the way from Pécs to nurse a partially paralyzed grandson, only to find him fitter than ever.

Paul's transformation, the mountains and the companionship heightened the enjoyment of the outdoors for both father and son. Family, sunshine and exercise in the mountains had overcome what even modern science could not. For the rest of his life, Paul remained skeptical about doctors' advice.

For the next two years, the family continued their seasonal migrations between Vienna and Altaussee. Winters in the city inevitably meant someone in the family had a cold or a minor throat or sinus infection, so no one was alarmed when, in the winter of 1896, Eduard developed tonsillitis.

The infection was untreatable – penicillin and anti-inflammatories were not available – but most patients recovered in a matter of weeks. Eduard's infection, however, developed into painful rheumatic fever, which threatened kidney failure, nervous disorders and infection of the heart valves. The family could do little besides offer Eduard salt water to gargle and laudanum to dull the pain. On April 21, 1896, Eduard succumbed to a coronary infection. He died at the age of 49, leaving behind a 39-year-old wife, a 9-year-old son and 12- and 13-year-old daughters.

For the Viennese, a *schöne Leiche* – literally a beautiful corpse, but in practice a beautiful funeral and grave monument – was considered important to the mourning process. Eduard, however, was buried in the Jewish section of Vienna's new civic cemetery, the Zentralfriedhof, located (despite its name) in the distant suburb of Simmering. It was, as yet, largely empty. Many feared that its family plots would look insignificant and anonymous. The Viennese joked that it was half the size of Zurich, and twice as fun. To counter this reputation, the city fathers capitalized on Vienna's fame as the city of music and dedicated a Zentralfriedhof section to musicians and composers. Too impatient to wait for modern greats to pass away, they reinterred Beethoven and Salieri there. Mozart remained in his mass pauper's grave but got a tombstone anyway. A year after Eduard's death, these greats would be joined by Eduard's friend Johannes Brahms.

Eduard's tiny funeral cortège followed the hearse past the musicians' section to a corner of the cemetery reserved for Jews. Vienna mayor Baron von Felder had fought the Catholic bishops to secure even a small and not very picturesque Jewish section. The princes of the church had originally demanded that the departed members of the city's 140,000-strong Jewish community be excluded from the Zentralfriedhof altogether.

At the graveside, the rabbi recited the mourning Kaddish in Yiddish. Paul's uncles would have repeated the stanzas. The lines reminded them of God's promise of a world where assimilation would be unnecessary. "May He establish His kingdom in your lifetime and during your days, and within the life of the entire House of Israel, speedily and soon; and say, Amen."

Eduard, an assimilated Jew who did not convert to Christianity, was buried in unconsecrated ground, like a suicide or apostate. Music newspapers as far away as London and New York mentioned his death, but he left no mark in the world of music. His scores did not survive. His theories were lost. None of his students became maestros.

Paul had lost his mentor, protector, teacher, healer and hiking companion. His uncle Sigmund would continue to play a role in his life as a benefactor and patron, but never as a companion and kindred spirit. Paul later wrote on a number of outdoor subjects, but he never mentioned his father, the first man to introduce him to the mountains.

Lina gave up on the city of unhappy memories and took her children back to Altaussee to mourn her husband. She never remarried. Over the next five years, Paul spent little time in Vienna. Between Lina's tutoring, whatever legacy Eduard had left behind and support from Uncle Sigmund, the family had a relatively comfortable life. They kept a housemaid, and in photographs the children are well dressed and have bicycles, expensive items at that time.

Paul graduated from the local primary school in 1898, at the age of 12, and began his studies at a *Gymnasium*, a high school for the best students. After eight years of hard work, a lucky, talented, tiny, minority of *Gymnasium* students would be allowed to write the difficult *Reifeprüfung* tests, which entitled them to the university entrance diploma known as the *Maturazeugnis*.

The *Gymnasium* was a painful rite of passage. Assignments included rote memorization of Latin, Greek, mathematics and history. Creativity and dissent were discouraged. Absences were allowed only in the case of grievous illnesses. Punishments for misdemeanours included floggings with a whip or a stick. The novelist Thomas Mann said the *Gymnasium* was a school for "a rather coarse masculinity; its youth spoke a jargon that was both brisk and slovenly; the vices condemned most categorically were softness and dandyism, the virtues that were most admired were prowess in drinking and smoking, physical strength and athletic accomplishment."[12]

Many alumni traced the birth of their animus towards society and skepticism towards tradition to the traumatic experience of the *Gymnasium*. Moritz Stiefel, a fictional student in Frank Wedekind's scandalous 1906 play *Spring Awakening*, excoriated the rote lessons, draconic discipline and competitive environment of the *Gymnasium*: "School makes me wish I was a cart horse! What do we go to school for? We go to school so that somebody can examine us! And why do they examine us? In order that we might fail! Seven have got to fail because the next class is only big enough for sixty."[13]

Viennese climber Eugen Lammer sputtered with hatred for the things he learned at the *Gymnasium*, and proposed nature as an antidote: "We smashed everything our fathers had taught us. We mocked all their wilted ideals, all that they considered good and beautiful and true, their architecture, their art, we denied their religion and their patriotism, any authority, marriage and, above all, tradition. I was not immoral, but amoral, like the oak, and the eagle, and the storm."[14]

With his sleepy, dark eyelids, crystal-blue eyes, long hands and clothes worn with the precision of a boy still checked by his mother before he left the house, Paul lacked the appearance of a rebel. With the approach of manhood, however, his boyhood languor gave way to a new intensity. In photographs, his eyes narrowed; his mouth, at rest, curved into something between a smile and a sneer. After Eduard died, Paul began to dress in Ausseer *Tracht*, the traditional adult male clothing of the *Senners* of Altaussee. *Tracht* included lederhosen (short trousers), a waistcoat and a jacket. Buttons were fashioned from deer horn or wood. The best of these garments were made from the tough, supple, windproof hides of local deer, dyed forest green. Many mountaineers adopted *Tracht* as climbing clothes. Paul wore it throughout his life, both on the mountains and in the city. The black and white photographs of the day do not show the deep forest green of his jacket, the gold of his watch fob, the blue and purple neckties he loved nor, for that matter, his blue eyes or shock of blond hair.

Style alone does not explain Paul's choice of clothes. In his *Gymnasium* years, Paul began to slip out of the house before the family had risen in the morning, to hike or scramble in the mountains alone. Modern climbers protect themselves with layers of technical synthetic garments made on the other side of the world, in styles determined by global marketing strategies. Before Paul went out into the alpine dawn twilight, he hid his Jewish body in garments dyed the hue of meadow grass and cut according to centuries-old Catholic traditions, from the game of the dark forests he would pass through to reach the peaks.

Before Paul had equipment or training, his *Tracht* stood between him and the mountain. Like the young hero Jacob in the Torah, Paul had disguised himself in the hides of wild beasts. When he donned a *Senner's* garb, he subverted the circumstances of his birth. For the rest of his life, he remained almost ritualistically fastidious about his clothes. Sophie noted that although he often returned from a climb with his suit in tatters, everything from his tie to his vest remained in its proper place.

He began to keep a diary of his climbing activities in 1906, but he later told his friends that in the course of his *Gymnasium* years, he made some 300 ascents, mainly on his own, although occasionally with his sisters or local kids like the Mittler brothers. It was a remarkable achievement for a young man who had no reason to believe himself capable of mountaineering.

Even more remarkable is that Paul found soloing psychologically difficult. Some soloists are born with a natural ability to suppress fear and resist distraction by the potentially fatal implications of the absence of a rope or a partner. Scans of the brain functions of modern soloist Alex Honnold, for example, showed that the fear centres of his brain were unusually hard to stimulate. Soloists sometimes say that their minds are clearest when they climb alone. Paul had no such luck. In 1912, he wrote that alone in the mountains, he was aware "both [of] the immense power of nature and the subtlest and most innermost impulses of [his] heart, the secret games... minds play." These thoughts "are obvious [benefits] and offer pure pleasures. To the extent that we climb with others, the value to our inner lives decreases."[15]

If Paul merely wanted to wander off on his own to enjoy nature at his convenience, he would not have tested himself against mountains. His father's death, sickness and religious marginalization had introduced a serious note to an otherwise carefree childhood. Solo, he played, half-consciously perhaps, a game in which he won round after round against death, the adversary who had taken his father. The prize was the continuation of his campaign to possess the local ranges, path by path, scramble by scramble, mountain by mountain. Thomas Mann wrote this of childhood games:

> These games, whose deeper meaning and attraction no adult is able to understand any longer and for which nothing more is needed than three small stones or a piece of wood, perhaps wearing a dandelion bloom as a helmet; but above all, the pure, strong, fervent, chaste, but still undisturbed and unintimidated fantasy of the happy age when life still hesitates to touch us, when neither duty nor guilt dares lay a hand upon us, when we are allowed to see, hear, laugh, be amazed and dream without the world's demanding service from us in return...[16]

Paul started on easy peaks but progressed towards ever harder and more dangerous objectives. Early ones, such as the Zinkenkogel, were barely peaks at all. Others sported geological novelties or legends known to every local child. Before Paul ever climbed, he knew that plants could not flourish on the Totes Gebirge, that there was a fountain of youth on the Grosse Bischofsmütze and that a stone cast into the magical hole on the Lawinenstein caused a thunderstorm.

Mina often accompanied Paul in the mountains. She later recalled that he liked to skip switchbacks on trails and hike straight uphill, clambering over any cliffs in his line of ascent.[17] Even as a boy, Paul was driven to raise the stakes. Eventually, for no known reason except that it was the logical extension of his mountain games, he decided to climb a real technical peak: the Grosse Bischofsmütze.

At 2458 metres *Adriahöhe* – or above the Adriatic Sea, as the peaks of Austria-Hungary had been measured since 1875 – the Bischofsmütze was considerable in height relative to the surrounding mountains. It was also the highest peak in the Gosaukamm group in the Dachstein, the subject of the painting in Paul's parents' bedroom and a well-known local landmark that had divided the domains of the prince-archbishop of Salzburg and the archduke of Austria. The single route to the summit climbed a steep gash in the mountain known as the Mützenschlucht, and had only been pioneered in 1879. It was a dramatic leap in difficulty from Paul's hardest summit scrambles.

Although the name of Paul's partner has been lost, 11-year-old Franz Mittler or his 12-year-old brother Otto, with whom Paul later climbed the West Face of the Trisselwand, are both possibilities. It says much of Paul's forces of persuasion that he could convince another child to join him on his first true technical climb, an unroped ascent of the vertical limestone tooth of the Grosse. It was the first but not the last time Paul concealed his climbing plans from his loved ones.

The boys snuck away from town and hiked up the Gosau valley to Stiegl Pass, a strenuous excursion up exposed rock slabs that verged on mountaineering. With no money to stay at the Hofpürgl hut and no extra equipment, the boys spent a long, cold night on the rocks. Paul learned from this first experience why the root of the word bivouac, *beiwacht*, meant not to camp but to stay awake and watch.

At dawn, they trudged up the talus to the Mützenschlucht, where the route began. Most boys would have realized the foolishness of their plan and turned back at the sight of the 330 metres of vertical rock that towered over them. Paul and his companion climbed the exposed route together but unroped, then downclimbed it.

Lina spent two sleepless nights at 53 Puchen before Paul returned. His story of the climb did not impress her. She had lost a husband to disease, and now she could have lost her son to a mountaineering prank. Uncle Sigmund surely warned the boy about the dangers of mountaineering. When Paul later wrote about how parents and authority figures react to young female mountaineers, he may have used anecdotes based on his own boyhood experiences: "The [young climber's] difficulties start in the valley, with the weary mother's thousands of ruses [to dissuade the climber]... Uncles will also discourage [them] by reading accident reports."[18]

The uncles in question would have had plenty of material. Top climbers often died young. Viennese alpine purist Emil Zsigmondy died on the South Face of the Meije in 1885. Mountaineering writer W.B. Coolidge called Zsigmondy irresponsible, but

Paul later hung his picture on his bedroom wall next to Georg Winkler's.

The son of a Munich pig butcher, Winkler climbed boldly and with passion. He was also a loner who kept a detailed diary of his intense emotions and scrapes with death on the mountains. He died alone in an avalanche on the Weisshorn in 1888. His diary was published in 1906 as *Upwards!* and became mandatory reading for young German climbers. Winkler achieved a cult status usually reserved for romantic, self-destructive characters like the hero of Johann Wolfgang von Goethe's sensational novel *The Sorrows of Young Werther*. To paraphrase Goethe, every romantic climber had a period in their life when they believed that Winkler had written just for them. "I have long been aware of the danger involved in my climbs," said Winkler, "and soon realized that it is, indeed, seeking out and overcoming this very danger that affords a climber unlimited satisfaction. The union of this danger with the infinite magnificence of the high mountains exerts an irresistible, demonic attraction."[19]

Instead of the corporal punishment suffered by most children, Lina locked Paul in his room until noon on weekends and deprived him of the daylight hours needed to reach the mountains. Paul secretly disobeyed her. He hid his rucksack in the garden in the afternoon, slipped out the window after bedtime, climbed by the light of the moon and the rising sun and stole back into his bedroom before Lina unlocked it at noon. When Lina remarked that Paul looked tired and dishevelled for a boy who had just spent 12 hours in bed, his sisters, especially Mina, vouched for him, although they knew the truth.[20] Lina soon lifted the punishment.

Mina enjoyed climbing and skiing, and became one of Paul's regular climbing partners. Sophie took a more traditional role and packed his rucksack, made his lunch and cleaned and repaired his climbing clothes for him.[21] From the beginning, Paul's sisters and Lina winked at or simply indulged his desire to climb as he pleased. Traditionally, a family's father – even a gentle one like Eduard – was the stricter parent. When Eduard died, Paul lost a controlling influence on his behaviour.

Paul had his own reasons to disobey Lina. Love motivated Lina both to ground Paul and to indulge his disobedient climbing. Either way, she stoked the fires of his boyish sense of invincibility and self-confidence. In this sense, Paul did not share Winkler's and Lammer's nihilistic aversion to house and home. For Paul, solo climbing affirmed his place in his home and the world, maintained an activity he had enjoyed with his father and added the thrill of risk.

Paul took the part of the leader when he and his sisters went into the mountains, but his sense of male privilege was conflicted. He knew banal details about women's cosmetics and some of the issues female climbers faced, but remained hesitant to credit women as climbers in their own right. He spoke of the importance of manliness but fussed over his own clothes, even when he was climbing. Hut custodians were impressed that he returned from hard climbs in bad weather with his collar still standing.[22]

At the same time, while most male climbers of Paul's generation rarely, if ever, climbed with women, Paul sought female rope mates of different abilities and backgrounds on a regular basis and wrote about them afterwards, always from the position of the superior partner. Austrian novelist Stefan Zweig spoke of a man like Paul as "twice as good, twice as much himself when he knew that women liked him, just as many actors find their most ardent vein when they sense that they have cast their spell over the audience, the breathing mass of spectators before them."[23]

In 1906, Paul reached the age of 20. He had survived a Jewish boyhood in the Catholic mountains of Styria, paralysis, the death of his beloved father, hundreds of impromptu climbs and the *Gymnasium* – and with the help of his father, and then his mother and sisters, he had flourished. Altaussee would remain his home base, but his acceptance into the vaunted University of Vienna took him out into the larger Austrian-Hungarian and German world.

Paul was not yet a climber by any definition besides his own, despite his love of the mountains. That would be life work he would undertake with those he would meet in Vienna, not the mountains of Styria. As for his field of study, his boyhood declaration of love for flowers and mountains had been portentous. He chose to major in plant biology.

The Student Mountaineer, Vienna 1907–10

As a young man, neither tennis nor golf interested me; to my mind in those days, any sport in which you could not kill yourself had no moral value.

—Martin Freud, *Glory Reflected*

Like most graduates of the *Gymnasium*, Paul had an impressive command of languages ancient and modern, and general knowledge of everything from history to arithmetic. The *Maturazeugnis* guaranteed a complete education.

The American writer Mark Twain commented on the lives of the fortunate few who went on to attend university:

> [They] have left the gymnasium with an education which is so extensive and complete, that the most a university can do for it is to perfect some of its profounder specialties. It is said that when a pupil leaves the gymnasium, he not only has a comprehensive education, but he knows what he knows – it is not befogged with uncertainty, it is burnt into him so that it will stay. For instance, he does not merely read and write Greek, but speaks it; the same with the Latin.... the German [or for that matter, as far as the *Gymnasium* is concerned, Austrian] student specializes in the nature of some specialty, such as a particular branch of law, or diseases of the eye, or special study of the ancient Gothic tongues. So this German attends only the lectures which belong to the chosen branch, and drinks his beer and tows his dog around and has a general good time the rest of the day.[24]

Paul was one of the small cadre of university students who intended to go on to graduate studies, because of either intellectual vocation or the lack of a family contact who could provide them with a job. It was up to each student to attend enough lectures in their four-year program to pass the examinations for the *Magister* degree required to continue to graduate studies.

Most students, however, went directly from the university, with or without a degree, into family businesses, government appointments, the military, or a life as a *Bummerl*, as the Viennese called an unemployed man engaged in aesthetic pursuits and typically living off a family income. Many patriarchs considered a few years in university a chance to sow wild oats before marriage and settle down, rather than a period of academic refinement. Low fees and professors' wages led to a pedagogy of indifference.

Mark Twain described the atmosphere at lectures:

> About a minute before the clock struck, a hundred and fifty students swarmed in, rushed to their seats, immediately spread open their notebooks and dipped their pens in ink. When the clock began to strike, a burly professor entered, was received with a round of applause, moved swiftly down the centre aisle, said "Gentlemen," and began to talk as he climbed his pulpit steps; and by the time he had arrived in his box and faced his audience, his lecture was well underway and all the pens were going. He had no notes, he talked with prodigious rapidity and energy for an hour – then the students began to remind him in certain well-understood ways that his time was up; he seized his hat, still talking, proceeded swiftly down his pulpit steps, got out the last word of his discourse as he struck the floor; everybody rose respectfully, and he swept rapidly down the aisle and disappeared.[25]

A student who wished to apply for graduate studies had to put in a year of self-directed study known as the *Grundstudium*. Even to enter the final phase of the *Diplom* degree, or the *Hauptstudium*, which entitled them to apply to graduate studies, the student had to pass examinations and write a thesis paper. The first two care-free years of undergraduate life did little to prepare them for the grind of the *Hauptstudium*.

Predictably, few students took an interest in graduate studies. Most were young men in their late teens and early 20s with little need of good marks. They indulged in marathon beer drinking sessions and duels. Corps, fraternities, clubs and societies prepared young men for male club membership, a mainstay of bourgeois male adulthood. Active and curious students like Paul often spent more time in extracurricular activities than at lectures and in libraries.

This is not to say that the University of Vienna was an academic wasteland. Important work in many fields was undertaken every year, at least by professors and graduate students. In Paul's field, for example, the International Rules of Botanical Nomenclature were drafted at the university in 1905. Paul, however, did not recall the content of his lectures with anything like the enthusiasm with which he described the camaraderie and thrills he enjoyed on the fencing, tennis and figure and speed skating teams.

Naturally, Paul's favourite student organizations were the mountaineering clubs, which were more geared towards the interests of alpine thrill seekers than *Bergfreunde*. Martin Freud, the least intellectual of the great psychoanalyst's children, was a university wastrel, a duellist with cheek scar to prove it, and later a climbing partner of Paul. A typical club climber, he wrote that "as a young man, neither tennis not golf interested me; to my mind in those days any sport in which you could not kill yourself had no moral value."[26] Freud recalled the excitement and danger he experienced in the university climbing clubs: "a friend of mine…. a voluntary guide to a mountain club… returned a number of times with a story but without his party. When he returned a third time during a few years' service with the embarrassing news that he was the sole survivor, the club decided to deny themselves of his services, a decision he accepted with great astonishment and hurt pride."[27]

Death, as the old saying goes, is a Viennese, and Austrian climbing culture was born in Vienna, as well as the Alps. In the 1930s, Martin Freud recalled the recovery of a fellow student-climber's corpse. "Very cautiously, we followed the direction of his fall, finding on the way his rucksack and boots, which, as is usual in such accidents, had been torn from his feet.... in the late summer, when the snow had melted, his body was found, perfectly preserved."[28]

Before university, Paul had never met anyone likely to have said that death in the mountains was preferable to boredom or compromise. In Altaussee, he had made his own, fanciful rules or simply climbed as circumstance required or allowed. After university, his creed included language common in Viennese circles about the acceptability of death as a possible outcome of mountaineering.

Paradoxically, Viennese mountaineers spent most of their time at a safe distance from the hills. In this salon-like environment, talking, philosophizing and writing about how and why to climb comprised an alpine discipline of its own. A few of these philosophers never ventured far beyond the Hausbergen and the writing desk, but some followed their principles to the death and became martyrs to an alpinism in which every climb must embody high (or, according to some observers, pitiless and foolish) ideals.

Viennese teacher Ludwig Purtscheller had championed the cause of guideless climbing, the first important stylistic challenge to the status quo of alpinism. The concept had been pioneered by British climbers in 1860s, although even the best British climbers continued to employ guides well into the 20th century. A few guideless climbing enthusiasts complained that some guides' unfitness and lack of modern climbing skills made them dangerous. The philosophical reason to do without guides, however, was that paying someone else to do the most dangerous climbing was unsporting.[29]

Purtscheller teamed up with brothers Emil and Otto Zsigmondy, fellow climbing-style idealists, for the brilliant unguided first 1885 ascent of the East Arête and traverse of the Meije (3983 metres) in the French Dauphiné Alps. In 1889, Purtscheller and Hans Meyer made the guideless first ascent of Kilimanjaro (5895 metres), the highest peak in Africa and the German Empire, a fine exploratory ascent for the era.

Purtscheller died of pneumonia in 1900 before he he had fully recovered from injuries suffered in a fall from the Dru in the Mont Blanc range in 1899. Emil Zsigmondy had died 15 years before, on the South Face of the Meije. Their legacies lived on in the essays, books and climbing reports that enshrined their amateur ideals, and in the climbs and words of the next generation. Viennese climber Eugen Guido Lammer, just 22 when Zsigmondy died, eagerly picked up the torch of climbing style. He survived many near-fatal accidents and helped found the *Austrian Mountain Newspaper*, the first of several climbing periodicals unaffiliated with clubs.

Austrian rock climbing authority Franz Nieberl was nicknamed the *Kaiserpapst* – or Pope of the Kaisergebirge (also known as the Wilder Kaiser), in the Northern Limestone Alps of Austria – for his encyclopedic knowledge of the climbing routes there. His pithy sayings, such as "you cannot reach the summit of any mountain in the Wilder Kaiser with your hands in your pockets," had entered climbing lore. The unaffiliated climbing papers were so radical that the *Kaiserpapst* put them under interdict and warned climbers not to read them in his popular 1909 rock climbing instructional manual, *Climbing Rock*.[30]

Viennese climbers ignored Nieberl's advice, spurred on by the amateur enthusiasm that filled the climbing papers. Austria was not as famous as the Western Alps or the Dolomites, and Austrian climbs received little attention from contemporary foreign mountaineering journals, but there was no lack of worthwhile achievements and hard climbers. Theodor Keidel, Thomas Maischberger, Heinrich Pfannl and Viktor Wessely's first ascent of the sustained 900-metre-high North Face of the Hochtor in the Gesäuse was a major breakthrough. Sepp Brunhuber's ascents of the 500-metre vertical wall of the Rosskuppenkante, the North Wall of the Hochtor and the Northwest Face of the Dent d'Hérens in Switzerland were major pioneering efforts in winter alpinism.

The striving amateur philosophies of Viennese mountaineering played no small part in these successes. The old term for the peasant guide was *Führer*, and the socially superior client was the *Herr*. This language ported the power relations of the *ancien régime* into the mountains. Guideless climbing culture inverted those values. The amateur leader took the front of the rope to prove his willpower, skill and sense of style, rather than to fulfill his class destiny as a seasonal labourer. The climber who followed was not the respected client, but simply *der Zweiter*, the second, who belayed the leader and acted as a witness – and later, photographer – of his feat. The lead climber became a figure of glamour.[31]

The school for this new breed of idealistic climbers was the climbing areas in the Hausbergen, mainly the Hohe Wand, with routes up to 250 metres high, and the shorter but steeper rocks of Peilstein. Before Willo Welzenbach introduced the first climbing grade system accepted throughout the Alps in the 1920s, a climb's difficulty could only be described relative to similar routes. In 1894, Peilstein guidebook author Fritz Benesch introduced one of the first climbing grading systems. Routes were graded I to VII. With the illogicality that became a tradition in climbing grades, 0 and 00 were reserved for the hardest climbs. Grades turned the Peilstein *Klettergarten* into a competitive playground and encouraged climbers to work their way to harder and harder climbs. Grades also allowed an out-of-town amateur like Paul to measure his skill against other climbers.

In-situ pitons were scarce on the Styrian mountains but, despite the philosophies of Purtscheller and Zsigmondy, commonplace on the crags of the Hausbergen. The increase in their numbers was partly a measure of the recent rise of commercialism in climbing. Although pitons had once been homemade or crafted by blacksmiths, mass-produced picture-hook and ring models were available on the shelves of fashionable outdoor stores like Mizzi Langer's on the Kaiserstrasse in Vienna. To entice climbers to pick up these items, Langer commissioned mountain artist Gustav Jahn to illustrate her catalogue with images of climbers using them. There is, however, a more obvious reason that pitons became popular. The leader's only other protection options were to drape the rope over a rock bollard, or tie it to a rock spike or chockstone with a sling.

The abandoned Rodauner quarry on the outskirts of town became a *Klettergarten*, as cliffs developed for rock climbing were called. It was known to climbers as the Mizzi Langer Wand. Langer even put together a demonstration climbing team known as the Langer Platte and held climbing competitions.

Paul had entered climbing just as the fascination with equipment and the possibilities it created became glamorous. According to Paul, even he temporarily fell under the piton's spell and climbed "loaded down with a metal-working shop and an ironmongery in each pocket."[32]

His pockets would have to be replenished occasionally, since soft steel or iron pitons conformed to the twisted cracks of the limestone rock and were next to impossible to remove. Despite Paul's description of pockets full of iron, so many pitons were in situ that few climbers brought their own.

The weakest link in the system was the connection between protection and the lead rope. The leader carried a dozen slings of four- to eight-millimetre-diameter hemp line in a jacket pocket to thread through a piton ring or loop over a bollard, then tie around the lead rope. If the leader fell, the friction from the static load of the 11- or-12-millimetre lead hawser could cut the sling. Ring pitons reduced the rope-on-sling friction, but to use one, the leader untied the rope from his waist, threaded it through the ring and tied it in again, a task for which a second lead rope came in handy.

Despite their crude safety techniques, climbers had pushed the standards of free climbing. By 1900, the *Klettergärten* of Vienna and Munich and the sandstone towers of Saxony had climbs of a standard only reached in Yosemite 50 years later. Some of the long routes in the Alps put up at this time have been quietly upgraded to 5.9 and a few even to easy 5.10.

Paul immersed himself in Viennese rock climbing culture. He read Purtscheller, Lammer and Zsigmondy, as well as the alpine papers. When he could not climb, he trained for rock problems by doing pull-ups on door jambs and a wardrobe. As he improved, however, he became aware of the difference between the high principles and the realities of climbing.

He observed that "young (and sometimes even old) climbers can be observed every Sunday in the Munich or Vienna excursion districts who, with blind trust in pitons and rappel slings, tackle the hardest routes without being even in the slightest equal to them and without knowing the correct use of those fine things [pitons] they have stuffed in their pockets... Prospective climbers should be instructed to keep their ambition within the levels of their ability."[33]

Self-reliance was part of the guideless Viennese aesthetic. Remembering all the climbs he had made without technical gear at home in the Salzkammergut, Paul concluded that the natural next step was to forgo pitons.

Paul had started climbing either as a soloist or the leader in a party of less skilled followers. Throughout his climbing career, with some exceptions, he continued to prefer such an arrangement. Tension only emerged in equal partnerships, or ones where less brave or skilled climbers took a leadership role. Consequently, many of the accounts of his climbing were written by less talented partners who were occasionally hyperbolic in their praise. Paul "climbed like the bird flew, or the fish swam. For him, it was like breathing," wrote Alexander Hartwich.[34] Partners closer to Paul in ability, although also impressed, were less overwhelmed by his technique.

In university, Paul found his first long-term friends, who also became his first rope mates. They were quick to recognize his talent as a climber and give him his first taste of the respect of bourgeois colleagues. Most of them had been raised by cultured, cosmopolitan parents. Most were Jews, or from families of Jewish immigrants from the provinces who had converted to Christianity in Vienna. His most famous partners were Martin Freud and his teenage sister Anna, who had taken many summer holidays in the Alps with their mountain-loving father. Martin was a keen climber and ski mountaineer, but he was just as enthusiastic about brawling with the bullies in anti-Semitic university clubs. Anna loved the mountains but eventually gave them up to pursue studies in psychoanalysis. The Freuds joined Paul often. Although Paul was neither a carouser and agitator like Martin nor an intellectual of the same water as Anna, the three of them became partners and friends.

Alexander Hartwich was a medical student two years younger than Paul. His Jewish grandparents had come to Vienna from the provinces at mid-century and changed their name from Hirschl. In 1884, a few years before Alexander was born, the Hartwiches converted, and Alexander was raised as a Christian.[35] Hartwich became a regular climbing and skiing partner of Paul's and a close personal friend.

Paul found his most kindred spirit in Paul Relly, a tall, handsome, serious law student who had earned the nickname Tiger for his aggressive climbing and skiing. Relly was a Jew and his father was a judge, like Paul's uncle Sigmund. When Relly Sr. had been called to the bar, he changed the family name from Rubenwurzel to the Christian last name of Relly, but did not convert.[36] Relly had grown up in the Vienna winter and mountain sports scene and was thus a good foil to Paul's self-taught native enthusiasm. Relly was Paul's most frequent climbing partner and closest male friend throughout his life.

Walter Schmidkunz was a year younger than Paul. He had grown up in a family of teachers and publishers in Kiel, on the shores of the Baltic Sea, far from the mountains. As was the case with so many German climbers of his time, he was introduced to the outdoors and the mountains by the Wandervogel (Wandering Birds) youth movement, a romantic, loosely organized initiative to get young people to hike and sometimes climb in the countryside. By the time Schmidkunz studied in Vienna, he was skilled and strong enough to accompany Paul on difficult climbs.

Paul had been raised with a cosmopolitan outlook, but Walter had travelled throughout Europe and worked in Italy and London in the book trade. Schmidkunz was a natural publicist, with his broad smile and curiosity. His pan-Germanic views were unusual in a Jew but made him less of a threat to non-Jews. Even as a student, he wrote for newspapers and experimented with the modern media of photography and film. In his capacity as an impresario, writer and publisher, Schmidkunz later introduced the climbing world to Paul and his ideas.[37]

Paul's first climbing partners had been his sisters, and recent changes at the university allowed him to continue to climb with women. The faculty of law had accepted women as students in 1897, the medical school in 1900. Some of Paul's female climbing partners, like Anna Freud, Jeanne Mauthner and Mitzi Pfeiffer, were brilliant members of the second pioneering cadre of women students. Emmy Eisenberg, an attractive, dark-haired climber whose father was a Jewish doctor in Vienna, became a frequent climbing companion of Paul's.

Acceptance into the lecture hall had not removed all of the obstacles facing women in university life. They were excluded not only from the duelling and drinking societies of the male student corps but also from most clubs. Women bored by the young ladies' religious and charitable clubs could find relative freedom and excitement in the mountains. The Alps were a rare place where young men and women could enjoy each other's company with little supervision, in pursuit of romantic or alpine objectives. Alpinists were not the first to discover the licentious potential of the mountains. "There is no sin on an Alp" was an old *Senner* saying.

The Wandervogel encouraged teenagers of both sexes to hike together without adult chaperones. Romance and sexual experimentation were inevitable and even encouraged. "Youth lasts only one night," wrote philosopher Walter Benjamin in the Wandervogel newspaper, *The Beginning*, "so let us fill it with ecstasy!"[38] Wandervogel culture abounded with such effusions, and scandalous rumours of wilderness orgies were published in newspapers, inspiring moral panic. Sigmund Freud loved the mountains but fretted about his daughters Mathilde, Anna and Sophie sleeping in mountain huts or climbing with anyone but family members.[39] Young people, however, flocked to the Wandervogel in the hope that the rumours were true.

Despite the traditions, rhetoric and rumours of alpine freedom, climbing itself remained a patriarchy. When women were not written or drawn out of climbing culture, they were often mocked as unstable rope mates with the potential to weaken male climbing powers through nighttime dalliances. Some 70 climbers appear in Carl Moos's illustrations in Nieberl's *Climbing Rock*, not one of them a woman. In the entire book, there is a single reference to the effects of bringing women to the mountains: a man who "surrenders to Venus" the night before an ascent, says Nieberl, climbs as a mere "half-a-man."[40] When women were praised in male climbing stories, it was typically for cooking or preparing camp, rather than participating as active climbing partners.

Paul climbed so often with women that he felt the need to explain himself to his mostly male audience in two articles in the climbing press, "Climbing with Women"[41] and "Putzi the Skier."[42] Both of these attempts to humour a male audience resort to sexist generalizations, innuendoes and omissions. "Good luck has led me to have shared my rope with seventeen different women," he wrote. "I will relate the joys and pains I experienced on these climbs. Although I risk losing the confidence of a couple of brunettes, blondes or redheads [by writing the article], I say, dear female climbing partners, each rule [about climbing] has its exception and you could be the exception."[43]

Besides his sisters, Anna Freud, medical student Grete Loew, Hans Dülfer's girlfriend Hanne Franz, German movie actress Lisa Fries, Italian guide Luisa Fanton, and, of course, Emmy Eisenberg, Paul had at least ten other women as climbing partners. He enjoyed climbing with women so much that Tita Piaz lured him into an attempt on the difficult unclimbed South Face of the Schüsselkarspitze by promising to bring Lisa Fries. The early 20th century, however, was an age of discretion, and gentlemen like Paul left few clues about the nature of their relationships. Only Emmy Eisenberg identified Paul as her "boyfriend for many years" and "greatest love," and that only decades after his death.[44]

Paul had grown up with the privilege of male gaze in a house full of women and had taken in a number of details of seeming importance to him. He knew, for example, the items they didn't need to bring with them on climbing trips – "concealer, lipstick, perfume, rosewater, nail polish,"[45] but his insights into their climbing motivations were facile and chauvinistic. Among other things, he said that women climbers were jealous and suspicious of one another, impulsive and prone to "total, paralyzing anguish."[46] He acknowledged, with sarcasm, that with careful training from men, women could become lead climbers.

"Women are the weaker sex?" he asked. "This assumption is called into question when one overhears the conversations [about hard climbs] of young women during dinner at the Hotel des Dolomites… New terminology and concepts only recently introduced in alpine literature are not lost on these women." He concludes with the implication that even women who know climbing exaggerate the difficulty of their objectives. "They interpret [climbs] in their own way. In terms of grading difficulty, they mostly stick to extreme descriptions."[47]

Paul ignored women's climbing records that he must have known well. Luisa Fanton had tried the North Face of the Campanile di Val Montanaia, one of the most difficult rock climbs yet attempted in the Alps. Hungarian sisters Ilona and Rolanda von Eötvös climbed a dozen new Dolomites routes, including the difficult South Face of the Grohmannspitze. German climber and pianist Käthe Bröske, along with Francesco Jori, made the first ascent of the Southeast Ridge of Punta Fiames, which was so difficult it was not repeated until 1922. British climber Beatrice Tomasson made the first ascent of the South Face of the Marmolada, one of the hardest walls in the Alps. Jeanne Immink, known to the Italian guides as *La Donna Instancabile* (The Tireless Woman), made 70 ascents, including the Grosse and Kleine Zinne, the first ascent of a new route on the North Face of the Cusiglio and the second ascent of the difficult Schmittkamin of the Fünffingerspitze.[48]

None of these women matched Paul's stereotypes, but Paul was not the only writer in this vein. Viennese mountaineering writers like Eugen Lammer embraced the sexist philosopher Friedrich Nietzsche. Most climbers, like Nieberl, proudly saw themselves as members of a spartan patriarchy that more or less completely excluded female partners. Paul's articles put an awkward, overly masculine gloss on his habit of climbing with women, as if to make up for a preference that other male climbers might call into question.

Paul's viewpoints seem strangely out of harmony with women's experiences of climbing with him. In an article in 1924 in the Bayerland Section newspaper, Emmy Eisenberg, who by then had climbed with many of the best climbers in the Eastern Alps, had much to say about the poor attitudes of men climbing with women. And yet she wrote that Paul was never sarcastic about her abilities, never falsely praised her, never expected less of her because she was a woman, and did not see attributes praised in men, like aggression and risk-taking, as negative in women climbers.

During his first year in university, Paul was preoccupied with the need to be accepted in male society and make his mark as a climber. In 1904, he purchased a small black notebook to use as a *Tourenbuch* (route book), but before 1906, he recorded few of his climbs. The first was the Schneeberg (2076 metres), the highest mountain of Vienna's Hausbergen. Along with the nearby Rax (2007 metres), this popular hiking and skiing peak became a mainstay of Paul's training. In 1906, he began consistently recording the names and dates of his climbs.

The Totes Gebirge and other ranges close to Altaussee were backwaters of Austrian mountaineering until the busy season of 1906. The first ascent of the 600-metre-high West Face of the Trisselwand by Karl Greenitz, Franz Kleinhans and Hans Reinl that summer was a psychological breakthrough. Paul made the first ascents of the North Face of the Däumling (2322 metres) with the Mittler brothers, and, in the fall, with a partner by the last name of Geiringer, the steep West Face of the Sandling. He also soloed the Trisselwand, the Eisenhut (2456 metres) in the Totes Gebirge and the Preber (2741 metres) in the Tauern range.

In 1907, Paul made his first visit to the Gesäuse range. The mountains were just a couple of hundred kilometres from Vienna, and a hut and trail system allowed convenient access to famous mountains such as the Hochtor, the Planspitze, the Tamischbachturm, the Grosser Buchstein and the Rosskuppe. Unlike the mountains around Altaussee, the Gesäuse was home to numerous prestigious climbs and often visited by the best climbers in Austria. A climb in the Gesäuse, which still contained many unexplored rock faces and ridges, would receive much more attention than one of the same difficulty in the Dachstein or Totes Gebirge. Here, Paul had his first chance to be noticed by the climbing world.

In the spring of 1907, Paul climbed some easy routes in the Gesäuse in winter conditions. On a short visit to the Altaussee in June, he soloed the Grosser Priel (2515 metres), the highest peak in the Totes Gebirge. When he returned to the Gesäuse, he made his first major enchainment when he linked the Tamischbachturm (1319 metres), the Kleiner Buchstein (1990 metres) and the Planspitze (2117 metres). He had intended to continue to other goals but was stopped by a storm in the steep canyon of the Peternscharte.

Enchainments were not yet popular or prestigious, but they gave Paul superb fitness and allowed him to maximize the opportunity of good weather. They also set the stage for spectacular enchainments later in his career.

On one typical weekend excursion to the Gesäuse, Paul and Relly climbed the Inthaler-Kamin on the Planspitze, in itself a successful weekend itinerary for most climbers. On Sunday, when Relly returned to the city for classes, Paul stayed in the mountains and soloed the East Ridge of the Hochtor.

Even when it rained or snowed, Paul charmed Martin Freud, Relly, Hartwich or Eisenberg into accompanying him on the Rax, the Schneeberg or the crags of the Hohe Wand or Peilstein. Despite rain, frozen ropes and wet boots, they recalled how bad conditions only heightened Paul's already considerable sense of humour and penchant for conversation.[49]

In 1907, Paul began to record some of his climbs in his route book in more detail, with notes about climbing style, difficulty and conditions as well as dates and partners. Like his hero, Georg Winkler, Paul had become a climbing diarist. Winkler's posthumously published diary revealed a glimpse into his psychology and personality, intended to be read only by the author. The surviving reproductions of the pages of Paul's climbing diary contain only a few words that stray from technical detail. One is a quote from the mountain poet Oskar Erich Meyer that Paul transcribed onto the first page: "We who look to the mountains search not only for beauty but for our souls. We believe that it is precisely the purity of the victor's cause that gains victory. The one who does not want to consider this trifles with his life; but he who consciously dominates the game, and accepts this truth, saying 'yes' to the game, does not. There are prizes worthy of the highest price."[50]

Paul dated the transcription – February 14, 1906 – as if it were a legal agreement to live by those words from then on.

In April 1907, Paul and some friends made what was, for him, a rare vacation to a destination other than the Alps: the Adriatic seaside towns of Fiume and Trieste.

In Trieste, Austrian, Italian and Slavic cultures overlapped, and the busy bars were home to a coterie of avant-garde intellectuals. Twenty-four-year old Irish writer James Joyce was finishing *The Dubliners* there when Paul and his friends arrived for their holiday.

Paul, however, never warmed up to cocktail bars or the seaside. After a few days, he quit the town to hike to the lookout tower on the rocky, grassy top of Vojak in the nearby Učka range, in modern-day Croatia. It was not much of a summit, reached as it was by a road, but Paul was more at home and more alive there than he could ever be on the beach. When, a few years later, he wrote that sport, which to him meant climbing, "for the idealist, is a way of life," he might well have had such a moment in mind. Even a scrubby hilltop nurtured him more than the most beautiful seasides in Europe.[51]

Schneid: Planspitze, Matterhorn, 1908

The measure of an alpinist's ability is not strength, but feline agility and Schneid.

—Emmy Eisenberg

The golden age of alpinism began with the second ascent of the Wetterhorn in the Bernese Oberland by Alfred Wills, in 1854 (hailed in England, incorrectly, as the first ascent), and ended with the first ascent of the Matterhorn, in 1865, by Edward Whymper, Lord Francis Douglas, Charles Hudson, Douglas Hadow, Michel Croz, Peter Taugwalder and his son of the same name. By the end of this 12-year period, the summits of most of the prominent peaks of the Swiss and French Alps had been reached. Austria, however, lagged behind the Western Alps. The Seekogel, for example, although a major Austrian mountain, was unclimbed until 1899.

There were plenty of challenging Austrian mountains, but they lacked the height of the Western Alps. Switzerland boasted some 30 peaks above 4000 metres, and France was home to the mighty Mont Blanc range, with the highest summit in Europe and several more peaks over 4000 metres. The highest peak in Austria was the 3797-metre Grossglockner. In the eyes of foreign climbers, like the British, who often referred to the Austrian ranges as "the lower Alps," Austria's mountains also lacked prestige. British climbing author R.L.G. Irving said that only climbers who had never seen the Western Alps were impressed by the Austrian mountains, which "have a slightly crushed, subservient look; you will not notice this if your mind is not possessed by the revelation of these greater, prouder [Western] Alps."[52]

Austrian climbers, however, made a virtue out of necessity and, lacking altitude, sought adventure and difficulty on hard, steep unclimbed routes. The trails and huts built for access to the easiest routes to the summits also gave unintended access to the unclimbed ridges and faces. Here, with a little imagination, lots of courage and perhaps a few pitons, an ambitious climber who could no longer find an untrammelled summit could find true adventure.

Although there were some substantially glaciated Austrian peaks, such as the Trafoier Eiswand, lower altitude meant that most alpine walls offered rock rather than ice difficulties. Austrian climbers, therefore, became rock specialists. In those early days of safety equipment, technical climbing on steep limestone faces required climbing skill, fitness, bravery and an adventurous attitude. The only information on climbing routes came through word of mouth or occasional trip reports in the alpine press. There were few good photos or drawings, and even fewer descriptions to help climbers find their routes. On one occasion, Paul and Hartwich searched in vain for an alpine rock wall they had seen only in a sketch by their friend, climber and painter Edward T. Compton.

Good, or at least lucky, route finding could be a matter of life and death. Loose rock had to be thrown off or avoided, and both leader and followers gingerly weighted all holds equally, lest one should break. The leader was exhorted never to fall, because in some circumstances, even a short fall might tear both climbers off the mountain or break the rope.

A lost lead climber rarely considered lowering off a piton or bollard on the rope. The main method of retreat was downclimbing, roped on the steepest sections, one climber at a time. The abseil had been invented by Jean Charlet-Straton in Chamonix in the mid-1870s, but climbers avoided it because ropes and anchors were unreliable. Even dry new hemp hawsers laid by artisanal rope makers were viewed with suspicion. The hemp fibres were weakened by the rain and snow that caused many retreats. Not surprisingly, descents were the occasion of many serious accidents.

With limited options for safe retreat, Viennese engineer Eduard Pichl and university professor Friedrich Panzer's ascent of the Northwest Face of the Planspitze in 1900 represented a serious commitment. The Planspitze was a typical summit in the Gesäuse, easily reached by a trail first negotiated by hunters, with a vertical Northwest Face as yet little explored by climbers. Panzer and Pichl's 1200-metre-long route overcame loose rock, steep cruxes and long traverses. Although brilliant Austrian guide Konrad Kain guided two expert clients up it in 1906, its reputation as one of the more serious climbs in the Gesäuse was undiminished.

It was by no means the type of climb typically undertaken by a solitary climber, yet Paul made the first solo ascent a month before his 22nd birthday, in July 1908. It was the most significant single climb in Paul's development as a climber since he had snuck off to the Bischofsmütze in 1897. The latter had proven that he was no longer just a dreamy schoolboy nature lover or a hiker. The Planspitze differentiated him from student alpinists like Martin Freud, who sought thrills rather than alpine mastery; it showed that Paul was, at least potentially, an alpinist of note.

The climb showcased Paul's skills, like applying his weight equally to each hold to minimize the chance of a fatal broken hold. When his extraordinary instinct for route finding erred, which it rarely did, he was an expert downclimber. Emmy Eisenberg exaggerated when she said that "the thought of danger never touched him," but not when she said he succeeded "because of his extraordinary technique and abilities."[53] Paul knew that the Planspitze solo was special. He listed it first on the 30 or so ascents he included in an application to the Austrian Alpenklub in 1908, with the note "*allein*," or alone.

"Although close ties of friendship and affection towards our climbing partners bind us," Paul wrote, "and soloing doubles the risk, it compensates us hundreds and thousands of times over."[54] Before the Planspitze, the compensations would have mainly been personal; after the Planspitze, they included the praise of other climbers.

What separated Paul from the many climbers who merely dreamed of making a climb like the Planspitze was an unusual amount of *Schneid*, loosely translated as guts. Franz Nieberl thought *Schneid* essential to climbing success:

Quite inconsistent with cautiousness… is another property that bold climbers must necessarily call their own if they really want to do successful rock work, and that is alpine *Schneid*. When we speak of a climber with *Schneid*, we want to say, "his heart is in the right place, he dares to do what he has to." Such a climber approaches every task on the rock with enterprise and sees it through with resolve. The opposite of this quality is indecision and a lack of energy and the lack of this vital force has often been absent from the start in parties who attempt a climb and fail within reach of the alpine laurel, which is soon after picked by parties with *Schneid*… Unfortunately, *Schneid*, in some situations, can also reflect a sense of personal insecurity and displace reason and recklessness ensues. Hotheads prone to this behaviour only escape death by the power of a benevolent fate. Many a hopeful life is broken on the cold rock because a climber lacked the real, measured and carefully considered quality of true *Schneid*.[55]

Some climbers reduced their reliance on *Schneid* with pitons and rope tension. Tyrolean traverses were already in the arsenal of many hard rock climbers, like Giovanni Battista "Tita" Piaz and Angelo Dibona, while Hans Dülfer introduced the tactic of swinging across holdless traverses on a rope. New techniques not only increased safety but made it possible to conquer previously unclimbable rock. *Schneid* went a lot further than it used to.

Paul did not solo the Northwest Face of the Planspitze for convenience, for speed or because it was easy. It was his first public demonstration of his intention to prove that the value of a climb resided not in the technical difficulty alone, but in the fact that it was done with an absolute minimum of technology. Such a statement required accepting of the possibility of death.

In the style of a Viennese *Bummerl*, Paul pursued his interests with a minimum of full-time employment, with only a couple of exceptions. Lina had worked in service to aristocrats and taught languages to their children. Paul, with his fine manners, education and languages, could have easily taken a part-time teaching position that would have left him time to climb. Pride and a sense of social ascendance into the bourgeoisie prevented him from doing so until the summer of 1908, when he took a temporary position as the German and French tutor of the children of a British lord. The location of the job was Zermatt.

A small town in Switzerland's Pennine Alps, Zermatt vied with Chamonix, France, and Courmayeur, Italy, for the status of the world capital of alpinism. Climbers and tourists from around the world came for its mountains and guides. Mark Twain visited in climbing season:

> … guides, with the ropes and axes and other implements of their fearful calling slung about their persons, roosted in a long line upon a stone wall in front of the hotel, and waited for customers; sunburned climbers, in mountain-eering costume, and followed by their guides and porters, arrived from time to time, from break-neck expeditions among the peaks and glaciers of the high Alps; male and female tourists, on mules, filed by, in a continuous procession, hotelward-bound from wild adventures which would grow in grandeur every time they were described at the English or American fireside, and at last outgrow the possible itself.[56]

The main attraction was the Matterhorn, the most recognizable mountain in the world. There were also dozens of 4000-metre-high peaks, including the Weisshorn, the Dom, Täschhorn and Lyskamm. Most of these mountains were easily 1000 metres higher than Paul's conquests in the Totes Gebirge, Dachstein or Gesäuse.

For Paul, the Pennine Alps was a giant step up the ladder of scale and commitment. Zermatt had numerous glaciers and extensive permanent snow and ice at altitude. Avalanches, such as the one that had killed Georg Winkler on the Weisshorn, were possible, even in summer. Snow and ice climbing as well as rock skills were required, and if anything, ice climbing techniques and equipment were more primitive than rock techniques. Traditionally, guides went first on snow slopes to cut footsteps and save the clients' strength. Unguided parties took turns hewing steps out front. Paul did all of the work himself.

Glacier travel techniques had remained the same for a century, and instructional books summarized all of the known wisdom in a couple of pages.[57] Parties preferred to travel in large groups to act as counterweights in case one of them fell into a crevasse. Large parties also had a better chance of hauling a climber out of a crevasse. The rope between climbers was kept tense to minimize the distance of a potential fall. Climbers crossed glaciers in daylight to avoid crevasses. A solo climber relied on luck and reading the glacier's snow cover, which required local experience that Paul lacked.

Undeterred, Paul chose as his first climb the North Ridge of the 4221-metre-high Zinalrothorn. The route was reached by traversing the crevassed Mountet glacier, and the climbing on the rock ridge proper was steep and icy. Paul's confidence turned out to be well placed. He climbed, then downclimbed the ridge, recrossed the glacier and descended to Zermatt in the same day; a strong first effort on a 4000er.

Paul rested for two days and set out for the Hörnli Ridge of the Matterhorn. The first solo had been made ten years before by German Wilhelm Paulcke, and solo ascents of the Matterhorn were still rare. The route presented few serious difficulties for Paul, however, and he decided to descend the Italian Ridge to traverse the mountain. After a cold, open bivy in Italy, he crossed the Theodul Pass and climbed the 4164-metre-high Breithorn, the easiest objective of his Pennine Alps itinerary, before descending to Zermatt.

Paul covered a lot of alpine terrain in five days, especially considering that he had taken two days to recover. His confidence in his own skills, willingness to spend a night in the open and relentless drive had tripled his experience on peaks over 4000 metres.

He returned to his mother's house in Altaussee in September and never took another position in the employ of an aristocrat again. In Altaussee, he made a series of bold solos that included the third ascent of Reinl's route on the West Face of the Trisselwand, the second ascent of the East Ridge of Traweng and an enchainment of the Grosses and Kleines Tragl and the Sturzhahn.

Paul's 1908 season proved that Lina had been prescient to allow her boy to climb. No one needed to be told there was something special about a young man who climbed the Matterhorn alone. From here on, Lina and Uncle Sigmund embraced Paul's new identity as a mountaineer.

In the fall of 1908, Paul invited Relly to come and stay with him at 53 Puchen. Hartwich, Eisenberg and many other climbing friends would visit and get to know his mother and sisters. Relly, with his assimilated Viennese background, was taken by the Preusses' affinity for the region and deep connections with the community, its people and its traditions. Lina cooked with pumpkin oil like a *Senner* housewife. The garden was filled with local flowers, and the family grew their own pears and runner beans. They observed local traditions and even dressed like Ausseers.

Like Relly, Sophie, now 25, and Mina, 24, were taller than Paul. They had dark hair and high cheekbones and were at once cosmopolitan in their manners and rustic in their traditional clothes. That fall, Relly and Mina began their romantic relationship.

Even Ausseers accepted the Preusses as bona fide locals and a proper bourgeois family. One aging *Senner* turned hut custodian described the general view around Aussee when she described Paul as both a "Kerl," meaning a solid local fellow, and "ein feiner Herr," or a fine gentleman.

At 22, Paul had begun his ascent to climbing fame, enrolled in a good university, passed muster with the *Senners* and bourgeois urbanites. He was a man in a man's world, free from the burdens of the proletariat, talented in his chosen field and loved by his friends and family. And yet, just then, he decided to take the final, most dramatic step in the process of assimilation and convert to Christianity.

Paul knew members of the Jewish minority who fought anti-Semitism. Martin Freud joined the Kadimah, a Viennese Zionist student organization that fought against the persecution and unjust treatment of Jews and worked for a Jewish homeland in Palestine. Famous Zionist intellectuals like Theodor Herzl summered in Altaussee. Most Austrian Jews, however, chose some degree of assimilation into Christian society rather than risk the conspicuousness of activism. Only a few went so far as to convert to Christianity, partly because even if their conversion was sincere, in the eyes of many Christians, a Jew remained a Jew, even after giving up their religion.

Yet this was the path Paul chose for himself.

Jesus of the
Dorotheergasse – 1909

We were in the midst of summer... a Sunday for the whole of nature.

—Paul Preuss

On January 30, 1909, Paul did not go into the mountains. He had forsaken the hills for his baptism at the Augsburg Confession Evangelical church on the Dorotheergasse in Vienna. This irreversible ceremony, at which he was the sole candidate that day, marked his conversion to Christianity and departure from the Jewish faith of his family.

Paul's reasons to embrace Protestant Christianity were rooted in his personality, friendships, family and a 400-year-old culture war between Catholic and Protestant Christianity.

In the Austrian Alps, the Catholic Church sanctified the passage of time in its rites for birth and death and rang the hours of the workday. Its crucifixes were planted on roadsides, meadows and mountaintops. As Paul climbed in the Totes Gebirge, he could keep track of the time by the nine strokes of the angelus bell that rang out from Saint Paul's church in Altaussee at six a.m., noon and six p.m. *Senners* stopped to recite their prayers in the fields at the sound of the bell.

There had been a time, however, when the Catholic Church was all but extirpated from the Styrian mountains. The Styrians were receptive to the ideas put forward by the Protestant Diet of Augsburg in 1530. By 1600, two-thirds of Styrians were Protestants. The famous Protestant astronomer Johannes Kepler taught at the Evangelical seminary in Graz, the capital of Styria.

Emperor Ferdinand II re-Catholicized Styria in 1629 and forced the nobility to convert to Catholicism or face exile. Farmers and peasants who would not convert had their property confiscated.

Protestant books and bibles in the vernacular were hidden, and Evangelical Christianity went underground for 200 years.

In 1821, Emperor Ferdinand I – the uncle of the emperor of Paul's lifetime, Franz Joseph I – took a more lenient view towards Protestants. In the municipality of Graz, which included most of the population of Styria, Protestants were finally permitted to build schools and churches, so long as they were modest structures without bell towers and did not compete in magnificence with Catholic churches. Franz Joseph, an even more enthusiastic promoter of religious freedom, promulgated the Protestant Patent of 1861 that allowed church towers and the organization of Evangelical dioceses.

Local and familial influences also played a role in Paul's choice to become an Evangelical Christian.

Lina's conversion to Judaism when she married Eduard set the precedent for religious conversion in the family. Although it is difficult to say how observant she was, her decision to convert was likely influenced by her desire to marry, rather than personal theology. Her pious Protestant youth and altruism comprised the spiritual foundation of her life.

She was not, however, the only attractive role model with a Protestant background that Paul could find in Altaussee. The rural Protestant revival in Styria was championed by industrious and dedicated clergy like the Reverend Friedrich Selle, the self-proclaimed "Austrian Alpine Pastor." Selle held earned and honorary doctorates in philosophy and had authored ten books on subjects ranging from Austrian history to anti-war theology and alpine botany. Selle became the pastor of Altaussee in 1902, where he remained until he moved up the road to Bad Ischl in 1922.

In his book *From Natural Knowledge to Christian Faith*, Selle explained that the human experience of nature could lead a soul to Christianity. He preached this gospel every Sunday at the Protestant church in Altaussee, which he had founded. Selle did not confine his interests to the pulpit. He also founded an Alpine Plant Garden Club that opened the public Alpengarten Bad Aussee in 1913. Selle's practical, scientific theology and his love of mountains and botany – and his proximity – would have drawn

Paul to him, and they were certainly at least acquainted with one another.[58]

Alexander Hartwich, who came from a family of converts, introduced Paul to Christian intellectual circles in Vienna. The philologist Elise Richter, the first female assistant professor at the University of Vienna, was unbaptized but attended church and renounced her Jewish roots. Lise Meitner, a beautiful and brilliant nuclear physicist, converted from Judaism to the Evangelical church in 1908. Like most converts, both women came from assimilated families and shared an attraction to uncompromising value systems and a hunger for tradition. In convert circles, Judaism was seen as the religion of decadent modernity and urban decay, whereas Christianity was seen as a religion of health, intellectual clarity and pastoral innocence. Paul's rural upbringing and love of the mountains provided fertile ground for such notions.

Between 1890 and 1914, the Austrian Protestant church grew by almost 100,000 members. Many new churches were built, including one in Bad Aussee. Conversion became fashionable among bourgeois conservatives, and many new Protestants were part of the nationalistic, anti-Catholic "Away from Rome!" movement. The majority of the membership of the German and Austrian Alpine Club, and thus most of Paul's friends and social contacts, were Protestants. The club's reputation for Protestantism led some Catholics to suspect that it intended to set up missions to convert the *Senners*.

The religious revival did, indeed, affect the German and Austrian Alpine Club. The Mark Brandenburg Section was founded in 1899 for Christian alpinists. In 1905, Christian mountaineers founded the Munich Academic Section, which refused all Jewish applicants and accepted "academically educated gentlemen of Germanic ancestry."[59] The national club, however, pressured them to remove the ancestry requirement. Although prominent Alpine Club members like Eduard Pichl thought nothing of expressing his anti-Semitic views in climbing journals, most anti-Semitism in the club was passive; good Jewish climbers were sometimes accepted as members and sometimes excluded for no apparent reason besides their religion. Paul, for instance, became a member of the Munich Academic Section, despite his ancestry, but was barred from membership in the Austrian Alpenklub (a separate organization from the Austrian and German Alpine Club) in 1908 by a majority vote, despite his outstanding climbing record. The application was turned down because he was a Jew and perhaps also because he took such unusual risks. Paradoxically, the symbol of the lone knight of the mountains who rose above the common man would later figure in the National Socialist conception of the new Aryan alpine man, but in 1906, it was considered anti-social.

Paul was a private man when it came to religion, but his friends observed a spiritual side that may have drawn him to the baptismal font. Emmy Eisenberg said he "approached the mountains with an exalted spirituality. The summits were like altars to him, and he embraced the alpine faith in its highest ethical and aesthetic form, in his quest to make solo ascents in perfect style."[60]

There was also a fiery, ascetic side of Paul that resonated with the Christian theology of sacrifice. He believed that mountains were to be accepted just as they were. To use pitons and ropes was to sin against that truth. There was a right and a wrong way to go about climbing. Better to risk death by staying on the right route than stray into error for the purpose of safety.

Paul's preoccupation with this sacrificial theme in mountaineering is illustrated in his handwritten inscription in the frontispiece of his route book, cribbed from German mountain poet Oskar Erich Meyer. The text follows in theme and structure, Saint Paul's exhortation in Acts 20:23–24, in which the faithful are told to run the race of life to win the prize of salvation. It was a Christian alpine creed.

Upon his request to be baptised, Paul was given a copy of Martin Luther's *Small Catechism* to read, with its commentary on the Ten Commandments:

> The First Commandment.
> Thou shalt have no other gods.
> What does this mean? – Answer: We should *fürchten und lieben* (fear and love) and trust in God above all things.[61]

The exhortation *fürchten und lieben* is repeated after each commandment. Paul's passion for the mountains was fuelled both by fear – of falling short of his ideals and the judgment of others – and by love for the mountains. The passage stuck with him.

He might have felt both of these emotions on the January morning when he walked from his apartment near the university, through the old Innere Stadt and the narrow defile of the Dorotheergasse, where the shadows made the cold bite harder. He passed the old city boundaries, which Jews had once been forbidden to cross. Even now, the city's main synagogue was hidden behind a false wall. He passed the neo-Gothic windows of Saint Jerome's Catholic church and the steepled, cream-coloured facade of the Stadtkirche, the temple of the strict Helvetic Confession Evangelical church, whose denomination he had passed up in favour of the less severe Augsburg Confession.

He made his way between the banks of empty pews into the baroque nave, where the morning sunlight from the clerestory windows glinted on the gold vault coffers, to the baptismal font near the front of the church. There, beneath the high altarpiece painting of Christ in agony on the cross, the pastor and the church warden awaited him.

The pastor poured water three times over Paul's forehead in the name of the Holy Trinity, and then he read Martin Luther's flood prayer:

> Almighty, Eternal God, Who, according to Thy righteous judgment, didst condemn the unbelieving world through the flood and, in Thy great mercy, didst preserve believing Noah and his family; and Who didst drown hardhearted Pharaoh with all his host in the Red Sea and didst lead Thy people Israel through the same on dry ground, thereby prefiguring this bath of Thy baptism; and Who, through the baptism of Thy dear Child, our Lord Jesus Christ, hast consecrated and set apart the Jordan and all water as a salutary flood and a rich and full washing away of sins: We pray through Thy same groundless mercy, that Thou wilt graciously behold Paul and bless him with

true faith in spirit, that by means of this saving flood all that has been born in him from Adam and which he himself has added thereto may be drowned in him and engulfed, and that he may be sundered from the number of the unbelieving, preserved dry and secure in the Holy Ark of Christendom...[62]

Paul had Christian friends who would have made sympathetic sponsors or godparents – roles required by tradition, if not canon law. But only the pastor and the church warden, Heinrich Klein-feldt, who signed the register as Paul's godfather, witnessed the moment in which Paul ceased, at least by rite, to be a Jew.

Some of the most obvious clues to Paul's spiritual inclinations are found in his articles about ski mountaineering. It was an emerging sport, but one which Paul pursued with passion.

For a third of the year, snow isolated small villages from tourists and gave the high Alps the appearance of a pristine wilderness. To the mountaineer, it was a world of unexplored spiritual, aesthetic and recreational possibilities.

Paul's descent from the snowline to a remote village was a spiritual experience, even for a young man raised amidst such sights. "Today, we pay attention to the crocus blossoms. The valley faces south, and suddenly, unexpectedly, we are in the midst of summer... it wasn't only a Sunday's Sunday, not even just Sunday for the country and the people in their Tyrolean clothes at the church, but a Sunday for the whole of nature, which had created a splendid, colourful festive scene."[63]

Paul was ideally situated to exploit developments in technology that allowed access to this untrammelled world. In 1888, Norwegian Fridtjof Nansen crossed the Greenland ice cap on an expedition that was criticized as impossible and foolhardy before departure and lauded in the press as a heroic adventure upon its success.[64] One of the keys to the expedition's efficient travel was the use of skis.

In Vienna, a Moravian artist and teacher named Mathias Zdarsky was intrigued by Nansen's adventures and tried out his own skis on the Hausbergen. Alpine skiers adopted the Norwegian practice of strapping sealskins on the skis to climb straight uphill without the inefficient herringbone ascent. The Norwegian bindings, however, were designed to traverse rolling plateaus and did not control the ski well on high-speed turns on alpine descents. Zdarsky developed a binding with a spring round the heel to hold the boot in place. Fritz Hullfeldt added metal toe pieces to give even more control through the forefoot, and the stage was set for the alpine skiing revolution.

In 1896, Austrian army officer Georg Bilgeri developed the ski with the central groove and the two-pole system. He also wrote *Alpine Skiing*, the first popular instructional book. Soldiers he trained to ski became instructors after their year of compulsory military service. Victor Solm set up the first ski school at Stuben in 1905, and other instructors followed his lead at Polsten, Arlberg, Kitzbühel and dozens of other slopes. The schools taught the newly invented stem turns, the telemark turn and the Nordic-style jump. Like metal edges, parallel turns were a thing of the future.

The huts that had lain unused through the winter made it possible for ski mountaineers to take their skills on multi-day trips over passes and up to the summits. In 1897, Wilhelm Paulcke pointed the way for long trips when he crossed the Bernese Oberland on skis. Finally, mountaineers had a winter outlet for their passion.

"Not so long ago," wrote Franz Nieberl, "winter held the mountains in deadlock, destroying all mountaineering plans, but this barrier has fallen today. The magic wand, which opens up to us the wonderland of winter, has been found in the Norwegian ski, which carries us almost effortlessly through the deep snow of the high valley up to the sunlit heights."[65]

Outdoor entrepreneur Mizzi Langer, always up for a new challenge in the mountains or the marketplace, used her fame as the sole female competitor in the first Austrian slalom race at Lilienfeld in 1905 to promote her range of ski gear. She found a receptive market among Viennese thrill-seekers and those who craved the solitude of the alpine winter.

Student mountaineering clubs organized tours, and Paul's

climbing partners Relly, Hartwich and Martin Freud were enthusiasts. From Christmas 1908, Paul began to record his ski tours in the same route book he used for climbing.[66] From then on, he spent as many winter days as he could on his skis. Much as he had used the outcrops of the Hohe Wand and Peilstein to hone his rock climbing skills for the mountains, he honed his skiing technique on the Hausbergen. On more than one occasion, he even participated in races. A photograph from February 1909 shows him wearing a numbered bib among skiers preparing to race down from the top of the chairlift on the Loser, near Altaussee.

In Altaussee during the Christmas holidays of 1908, Paul toured so much that his mother and sisters could not have seen much of him during daylight hours. On Christmas Day, he skied ten kilometres to Hallstatt, then traversed the Schneiderkogel. On Boxing Day, he explored the mountains around the Aussee. On December 30, he skied up the 2200-metre Alpkogel. In the winter of 1909–10, he skied in Altaussee every weekend between Christmas and the Easter break, touring the Totes Gebirge and climbing to the summit of the highest peak in the range, the 2515-metre Grosser Priel.

In 1910, Paul made a series of ambitious tours that pushed ski mountaineering in Austria to new limits. For his first major tour, he teamed up with Relly and Hartwich for a nine-day traverse of the Silvretta range on the Swiss border. In addition to weaving a course around 70 peaks over 3000 metres that crossed numerous glaciers, they climbed the highest summit in the range, 3312-metre Piz Buin, and six more 3000-metre peaks.

On April 10, the trio set out near the Wildspitze of the Ötztal range on a 60-kilometre trek across five passes above 3000 metres. Poor visibility and the winter snow cover on the Mittelberg and Taschach glaciers made for difficult route finding on the first day. Relly said that despite the weather, Preuss was always in a good mood and had a natural eye for choosing a path through crevasses. It was an important skill, as crevasse rescue, especially on skis, was in its infancy. The only time Paul broke through a crevasse, all that stopped him from falling into the glacier was a ski jammed across the opening. He flipped upside down so violently that he lost his rucksack in the depths.

After the traverse, an exhausted Relly and Hartwich headed for Vienna for well-earned rest. Paul, however, made a double ski traverse of the glaciated 3666-metre Grossvenediger, and followed it up with the first ski ascent of the Grosser Geiger and three other 3000-metre peaks. With or without partners, Paul was on his skis almost every day the hills were in condition. The cold, the solitude, the ascetic exhaustion in a desolate, frozen landscape high above quaint villages returned by winter to their medieval isolation – this appealed to him almost as much as the death-defying acrobatics of rock climbing.

In winter, climbing stopped, Alpine Club huts stood unvisited except by skiers, and hunters took to the mountains. Hunters combined the zeal of the arriviste with traditional privileges and unregulated firearms. The Austrian mountains had always been home to the red deer, boar and mouflon, and over the centuries, the elites had secured the sole rights to hunt them. In 1848, however, the restrictions that forbade commoners to hunt were lifted. In the craze to participate in what had been an exclusive privilege of aristocrats, hunting lodges and clubs proliferated.

In the Joh. Springer's Erben hunting store on Vienna's Josefsgasse, once the exclusive salon of aristocratic huntsmen and gun fanciers, middle-class would-be huntsmen admired the stuffed tigers and cheetahs. Photographs of aristocrats in the Alps or in African colonies, with their bearers and dead quarry, hung above cases of bullets, cartridge belts and pistols. This atavistic, masculine, colonial image of blood sport in the Alps stood in stark contrast to the athletic outdoor culture of Mizzi Langer's store, but it soon attracted an enthusiastic and growing cadre.

By the late 19th century, 7 per cent of the land in Styria had been purchased, appropriated or licensed for hunting. Peasants and their livestock were sometimes moved to villages to make way for red deer, which in many areas soon outnumbered cattle.[67] By any measure, the hunters' bags were enormous. The archduke Franz Ferdinand, for instance, had killed 5,000 red deer, not to mention mouflon, chamois and wild boar.

The months in which most of this game was hunted coincided

with ski season. Unsuccessful hunters accused the skiers of chasing away the game and interfering with the chase in other ways. Paul addressed the concerns of hunters in Schmidkunz's periodicals, *Winter* and the *German Alpine Times*.[68] "There are, of course, many amateurs in skiing, who are said to be prejudiced by the interests of the skiers," he said, "but these reproaches are unfounded... [amateurs] remain confined to places unsuited to hunting. One never sees amateurs very far from their hotel." Hunters had nothing to fear from skiing, he wrote, because "in the peaceful reserves of hunters who are friends of nature, not hunters who only hunt to be seen with a rifle, one meets only elite skiers, the disciplined and well-educated people who know the rules of hunting."[69]

Hunters boasted that their sport fostered military virtues like discipline, fitness, perseverance and, of course, shooting skills. The German word *Jäger* described both hunters and light infantrymen. Ernst Enzensperger, who had started an alpine youth movement in the German and Austrian Alpine Club, claimed that mountaineering prepared young men to be soldiers.[70] The Austrian army trained soldiers to ski, and Paul made the reasonable claim that curtailing skiing would decrease national military readiness because the sport contributed to physical fitness. "To hinder skiing, and precisely high-altitude skiing under the pretext of defending the hunt, is to attack the national interest," he argued, "since the wellness of the nation resides in the strength and physical fitness of its people."[71] Paul did not add that, despite being an avid skier, he had failed the physical test for compulsory military service.

Hunters had also complained that skiers frightened their quarry away and reduced their numbers overall. Paul objected that skiing helped the game survive because the chamois used ski tracks both as trails and to reach the buried pasture grass.[72] He expressed a spiritual and almost childlike love of animals. Skiers, he said, love game and would never scare it away; the true culprits were "teenage farmworkers, foresters and poachers."[73]

Hunters, however, were not the only vocal opponents of ski touring. Many members of the Alpine Club – "weird little owls who sulk and shout loudly at the 'board hoppers'," in Nieberl's words[74] –were concerned about the effects of the new sport on their precious huts and trails.

Older alpinists said skiers were less interested in nature than in the thrills of downhill rides. The sections had made massive investments in the hut system. Skiers, often younger than club members, used the huts in the off-season, when there was no custodial supervision. Rowdy ski weekends led to vandalism and careless damage. Repairs after the winter season made insurance so expensive that some sections went bankrupt.[75]

Enterprising sections saw an opportunity and winterized their huts, hired off-season custodians and encouraged groups of skiers to book paid weekends. Other sections kept their huts primitive to discourage skiers. Nieberl would have described a climber named Reuther from the Berlin Section, who proposed just this, as a "weird little owl."

"We older climbers used these primitive huts for forty years," Reuther complained, "with two lights from small lanterns, dry, cold bread from the backpack and a sip of brandy to warm you up on a cold summer night. And in the morning, with clothes still wet and wet shoes we set out once more on the unpaved path up to the peak. Sometimes we faced delay caused by weather, and sometimes we did not have enough food. But we were proud to have reached the goal and look back on the hardships we had to overcome... These skiers should be satisfied with what they get, which is more than we got in the [18]70s."[76]

Paul, however, argued that primitive huts were inadequate for ski tourers, and less than they deserved. He wrote that

> keyholes are blocked with snow and ice and I cannot get the key in. A good greasing would be an efficient way to get rid of this inconvenience. There should always be a vestibule outside of the locked door that is accessible by [an unlocked] doorknob. This door should not self-lock, as I have found myself locked out of a hut accidentally in the Stubai [Alps]. In this vestibule one could leave skis and wet equipment. Too often are the wool sheets in the dormitory so dirty that

they disgust even the winter athlete. The cutlery tends to be quite disgusting.[77]

He followed with a request that must have annoyed the likes of Herr Reuther: "I find very few pairs of slippers in huts, a piece of equipment that is so nice to have it is almost indispensable. Coming from a skier who carries 20 kilos on his back, it is a high task to ask that he carries slippers with him as well."[78]

Slippers were a modest comfort set against the harsh conditions of early alpine ski touring. The price of the spiritual enlightenment gained on dazzling snowfields was the mortification of the flesh. Even life at the huts could be brutal. Biographer Severino Casara claimed that on one of Paul's climbs, the thermometer at the Kürsinger hut on the Grossvenediger read minus-60 Fahrenheit.

The loads were crushing, the food was terrible. Martin Freud wrote that "each of us carried a hundredweight of food and equipment. We lived largely on dried foods, like Arctic explorers. One day we shared a primitive alpine hut with two Italian mountaineers. They had decided to cook for their meal a piece of raw meat which they had carried in a rucksack for several days exposed to the fierce rays of the sun…. They both concentrated their gaze on the meat for some moments without making a move to eat it. At last, the older mountaineer turned to the younger and said, 'Coraggio Casimiro!' and carved himself the first helping."[79]

Freud must have told the story to his father, Sigmund, for the great psychoanalyst referred to "Coraggio Casimiro!" as his "Italian motto," and used it often in his letters to his colleagues.[80]

It was difficult to maintain a clean, civilized appearance on a ski tour. "Heavily laden with food, skiing equipment and alpine gear," wrote Freud, "I had not had room for much toilet gear nor for any change of underclothing. Thus, unshaven, my face and neck covered with sunburn sores and my shirt in a frightful condition, I was not an attractive picture. I was joined on the road [at the end of the tour] by a real tramp, who looked quite neat and tidy compared with myself."[81]

Reactions to the concerns of ski tourers like Paul and Martin

Freud were mixed. The next time Paul spoke to the issue in *Winter*, he did so under the pseudonym P. Schulze.[82]

The skiers, however, eventually won the struggle against both the hunters and the traditional mountaineers. The Great War imposed restrictions on hunters, and most club sections winterized their huts. At the same time, the first ski resorts with hotels and groomed downhill trails were introduced. The first ski lift in the Eastern Alps was built at Bolzano in 1908. These facilities appealed to the skiers who had become unwelcome at the huts, and ski touring, once the only way to get to the top of downhill runs, became the preserve of dedicated ski mountaineers.

As if to further annoy the opponents of skiing, Paul championed both amateur skiers and professionals. In 1913, when a proposal was made to exclude ski instructors from competitions, he objected. He made fun of amateurs preoccupied with the technical details of waxing, a skier's speed on certain runs, or distances jumped, because, he said, he was a ski mountaineer who didn't trifle with such things to the same degree as a resort-based skier. Paul also wrote, however, that professional ski instructors should not be excluded from races on the basis that they were "socially and ethically inferior."[83]

For Paul, skiing, like climbing, should be a meritocracy. "Sport," he said, "for the idealist, is a school of life."[84] This principle was not at odds with his spirituality. Sport was a microcosm of the great contest: life itself. All were called to participate and all should have equal chance to win, including outsiders.

A crisis might have awaited a less motivated young man than Paul when he faced his final examinations in the spring of 1909. After all, throughout his undergraduate years, he had devoted more of his time to sports than books. His tour book shows that it was his habit to climb or ski in any available free time, and to extend his climbing weekends into the school week while his friends returned to the study halls. Nonetheless, Paul's desire to graduate was strong. He completed his work, temporarily changed his ways and spent hours in the university library, studying for his final examinations and writing his thesis paper. He passed his examinations and received his *Diplom* – and then, for the first recorded time in his life, he was unsure what to do next.

Instead of enrolling in graduate school, Paul used a gift from "a free-thinking uncle," as Casara described Sigmund, to fund a break from his studies. This wasn't just an extended climbing holiday; 1909 was one of the least productive climbing years of Paul's life. He restricted himself to the Dachstein and Totes Gebirge, climbed with partners more often than he soloed, and recorded few difficult new routes. In August he made a trip to the Silvretta range and bagged some easy 3000-metre peaks. In December he made an early-season ski mountaineering sojourn to the Rätikon range in Switzerland, near the Austrian border. None of these excursions included ascents as ambitious as the Planspitze, Zinalrothorn or Matterhorn solos.

It was a time of rest and reassessment after the changes wrought by his Vienna years. He had become a serious climber, found love and lifelong friends, changed his religion and earned a university degree. Like many of his era's artists and explorers, he was privileged to pursue his passions by his gender, education and bourgeois class, but he was also a prisoner of its obsessions with marriage, patriarchy, family, career and the respect of less adventurous or creative men. The path he chose was, in the end, the most predictable one. In the spring of 1910, Paul enrolled in graduate studies in plant biology, with the goal of becoming a university professor.

As if coming to this decision had temporarily dammed up whatever energies Paul needed for climbing, in the summer of 1910 he burst back onto the mountains with unprecedented fervour and creativity.

Dolomites: The Devil's Lair, Summer 1910

One must always do what the Devil forbids.

—Martin Luther

I n August 1910, when Preuss was 24 years old, he and Paul Relly made their first visit to the most famous centre of rock climbing in the world: the Dolomites.

In 1867, Austria-Hungary lost the Seven Weeks' War and ceded its ethnically Italian lands in Venetia to Italy – fatefully, though, the emperor retained the Welschtirol and the Dolomites. The people of the Dolomites were a mixture of Italian, Tyrolean and Ladin, the latter an ancient culture with its own language; the consequent use of both German and Italian names for the peaks can be confusing.

Geographically, the Dolomites comprised a number of ranges, including the Sella and the Marmolada, named after the region's highest peak, which was just 3343 metres and therefore lower than the Grossglockner. Most of the ranges offered good climbing, but the ranges of most interest at the turn of the 19th century were the Langkofel group, home to the Grohmannspitze, Innerkoflerturm, Fünffingerspitze and Langkofel (in Italian, Sassolungo); the Catinaccio (or, in German, Rosengarten) range, with the Vajolet Towers, Punta Emma, Campanile Basso, the Croda di Davoi and the Catinaccio itself; the Sesto Dolomites, near the Drei Zinnen, or, as they are better known to modern climbers, the Tre Cime di Lavaredo. None of these peaks were very high compared even to the Austrian Alps; their attraction to climbers was not altitude but topography.

The Dolomites are made of carbonate limestone rock that is loose in places but provides handholds, even on the very steepest rock. Erosion sculpted the ranges into bizarre pinnacles, walls and ridges that beckon to intrepid technical climbers. Even seasoned alpinists like Englishman Leslie Stephen were at once entranced and intimidated by the weird, vertiginous topography. "I was fairly perplexed and bewildered," Stephens wrote.

On every side there were gigantic cliffs, soaring pinnacles, and precipitous ravines. They rose so abruptly, and apparently in such wild confusion, all perspective was so hopelessly distorted, that I was totally unable to get my bearings. The fantastic Dolomite mountains towered all around me in shapes more like dreams than sober realities; they recall quaint Eastern architecture, whose daring pinnacles derive their charm from a studied defiance of the sober principles of stability. The Chamouni [sic] aiguilles, as I have said, remind one of Gothic cathedrals: but in their most daring moments they appear to be massive, immovable, and eternal.[85]

The climbing potential of the Dolomites had been discovered in the 1860s by Viennese student and founding member of the Austrian Alpine Club Paul Grohmann, after whom the Grohmannspitze was named. Over the last three decades of the 19th century, the Dolomites attracted a different kind of climber than the heroic adventurers and guides of the golden age of mountaineering in the Western Alps.

Most of the highest summits of the Western Alps could be reached by routes with at least some easier climbing, but Dolomites climbers focused on isolated pinnacles and walls that favoured visionaries willing to employ innovative rock techniques. A teenaged Georg Winkler used a grappling hook on the first ascent of the Vajolet Tower that came to be named after him. Jeanne Immink, Käthe Bröske, Beatrice Tomasson and the Eötvös sisters took women's climbing to new levels of difficulty in the Dolomites. Antonio Dimai, Angelo Dibona, Tita Piaz and Luisa Fanton represented a new breed of tough, locally born climber-guides whose talent and aggression in the Dolomites won them fame and a degree of upwards social mobility.

In 1910, the strongest local was Tita Piaz. That summer, Paul learned about Tita's skill, commitment and eye for a line by climbing his routes. The rock could not lie about Tita's character and ability, but the legends passed around the huts at night, about Tita and how he had earned the nickname the Devil of the Dolomites, blurred the line between legend and fact.

Giovanni Battista Piaz was born in 1879 in Pera, an ancient Ladin village in the Fassa valley, in the shadow of the Catinaccio group – a playground for hard climbers. The two biggest buildings were the medieval church of Saint Lawrence and the almost equally old Gasthof Sonne.

Tita came from a family of mountain labourers, and at least when it came to politics, he never forgot their plight. But from an early age he had something more exciting than manual work in mind for himself. When his parents sent him away to school in Bolzano, he took advantage of the first opportunity presented to him and neglected his books to become an excellent gymnast.

According to one legend, 12-year-old Tita won a bird in a cage at the Pera Easter fair. When he opened the cage to feed the bird, it flew to the top of a boulder the villagers called the Sass de Salin. Without a second's forethought, Tita scaled the rock to retrieve his bird. No one in Pera could remember anyone who had climbed the Sass de Salin, perhaps partly because it took its forbidding name from the pillar of salt Lot's wife was changed into after she looked back on the destruction of Sodom. When he came down, his mother asked him how he had scaled the stone and whether he had been afraid. "No," said Tita, "I just wanted to get my bird."[86]

The rescue awakened an urge to climb. Soon Tita was in trouble for climbing the bell tower of Saint Lawrence's church. Tita's mother tried to punish him by putting him under a box and sitting on it, but he burst out and threw her to the floor. His confidence grew out of proportion to his actual abilities on real mountains. At 14, he tried and failed to reach the Forcella di Davoi, although it was little more than a scramble. He followed this misadventure with an attempt on the Catinaccio d'Antermoia, the highest peak in the Catinaccio group; predictably, this also failed. Tita was not discouraged. He blamed his failures on "the jitters," but said that "at that young age, I proved to have a certain knack for balance."[87]

When Tita was expelled from school for refusing to make his confession, he spent most of his scholarship money on a drunken Christmas party. His first attempt to get a job was an audition for a position as a singer that he failed because, in his own words, he sang like "a swan lost on an iceberg" – not because he lacked a good voice but because he was hungry. He had gambled away his last food money at the billiards table the day before. He also failed his mountain guide's test, which he described as an exercise in servility. "A failed test, an empty stomach, and expelled from school," he said; "how life is hard and the horizon bleak!"[88]

By the time Tita was 20, he had embraced anticlericalism, socialism and irredentism (the movement to unify the Italian regions of Europe into a single country). Uneducated, marginalized and penniless, he returned to the Fassa valley and sought fame climbing the mountains he had known since he was a boy.

His first notable success was a solo ascent of the Winkler Tower of the Southern Vajolet Towers, a group of vertical 150-metre-high limestone pillars in the Catinaccio group. Although the Vajolet Towers were small next to the big walls of the surrounding peaks, they were easily accessible from the Leipzig Section's Vajolet hut and became a centre of hard-rock climbing in the Dolomites. From the beginning of their short climbing history, the towers had attracted only the most technically minded climbers. The Winkler Tower had been considered impossible until 1887, when 17-year-old Georg Winkler soloed it with a grappling hook and a rope cut halfway through by rockfall. An ascent of Stabeler Tower by H. Helversen and Hans Stabeler followed in 1892. The Delago Tower was climbed in 1895 by H. Delago. When Tita started climbing, the tower that later bore his name was unnamed.

Tita's Winkler Tower solo was reported in newspapers across Europe, and Luigi Rizzi, a famous guide who counted the king of Belgium among his clients, came to Pera to congratulate him. The attention convinced Tita to become a guide. "Life and society can often be cruel," he said. "I asked for nothing more besides the right to the simplest life, nothing but a job and bread, I, who adored nothing more than fresh air and the mountains, I, who craved nothing more than mountain tops, luminous horizons and limitless freedom of body and spirit."[89]

Because of his failed exam and his refusal to take it a second time, Tita was barred from advertising his services as a guide. His fiancée, Maria Rizzi, the daughter of the Vajolet hut custodian, helped him out and discreetly directed climbers in need of a guide towards her beau. Many of these clients wanted to climb routes that were too difficult or dangerous for legitimate guides. Tita's very first client demanded to be taken up no less a climb than the Winkler Tower, which, after all, was the source of Tita's reputation.

Tita took his rogue status in good humour and touted it as a benefit for clients who wanted to claim that their ascent was, technically, unguided. He refused to hide his politics from well-heeled conservative clients, however, and loudly sang "The Internationale" as he climbed.[90]

Tita's growing list of hard climbs served as his main guiding credential. In 1900, he made his most daring technical climb, the solo first ascent of the Piaz Crack on Punta Emma, a crack in a 300-metre vertical wall on a spur of the Catinaccio massif that he named after Emma the cook at the Vajolet hut. It was hailed as the hardest climb in the Dolomites. Soon afterwards, he made the second ascent of the Delago Tower, the sixth ascent of the Campanile Basso and new routes on the Piaz Tower.

In 1903, Tita married Maria Rizzi, and soon they had two children, whom they raised in the Vajolet hut. Despite his new responsibilities, Tita acquired a motorcycle and drove it recklessly enough to gain a reputation with the police as a dangerous driver; he also found himself in frequent rows with the hut owners in Germany over his responsibilities.

The rumour that Tita did not differentiate between rope tricks and real climbing originated in 1908, when he threw an iron ball on a rope over the summit of an unclimbed pinnacle and made a Tyrolean traverse to the summit. He named the pillar Guglia Edmondo De Amicis, after an Italian socialist and irredentist writer whose books Tita admired and whose son, Ugo, was Tita's friend and climbing partner. When Edmondo died, in 1908, his books became unpopular. By naming the pinnacle after his friend's father, Tita memorialized him in the best way he knew. Tita never considered himself the first ascensionist of this pinnacle; he willingly conceded that honour to Hans Dülfer, Willy von Bernuth, E. Kasnapoff and A. Zelger, who climbed it in 1913.

Around this time, with his craggy face, piercing eyes, Vandyke beard and climbing reputation, Tita acquired the nickname Devil of the Dolomites. "In the Fassa valley, and beyond," he said, "a legend was born: Piaz had made a pact with the devil. No one knew exactly which one, Beelzebub or Azaroth, but it was definitely with a high-ranking demon of Hell's hierarchy."[91] Tita claimed his beard and moustache were so menacing that not just climbers but women and children began to fear him. Each difficult new route and reckless run to town on his motorcycle added a layer to the myth.

On the Torre Principale, Paul and Relly's first Dolomite climb, Paul joked and sang. "I was normally taciturn," said Relly, "but [Paul] was so joyful, I joined in with him."[92] He was amazed by Paul's ability to read the rock and anticipate the path of the route, despite never have climbed in the Dolomites before.

The mood became more reflective when they decided to climb the Winkler Tower. The night before their climb, Preuss stood silent at the hut window, doubtless lost in thought about his hero, and watched the crescent moon rise over the Vajolet Towers.

On his first day on the Vajolet Towers, Paul climbed as if possessed. In a single day, he and Relly disposed of the Winkler Route, then the South Face of the Stabeler Tower, known as the Fehrmann Dihedral, first done a year before by German Saxon rock ace Rudolf Fehrmann and American Oliver Perry-Smith. Finally, they climbed the Piaz Tower. Counting the downclimbing descents they made of each tower, they covered some 1200 metres of vertical technical climbing. On their second day in the Dolomites, the two young climbers had turned the dreaded Vajolet Towers into a *Klettergarten*.

After the Vajolet adventure, they moved to the Langkofel group and had an easier day on the regular route on the Sassolungo. For Preuss, it was a short rest, and he followed up with an astonishingly long and bold solo traverse of the Sassolungo, the Fünffingerspitze and the Grohmannspitze. After the Sassolungo, he joined up with Relly for the first ascent of the steep, 400-metre-high South Face of the Grohmannspitze.

Of all the routes Paul did that summer, however, none influenced him as much as he and Relly's second ascent of the Piaz Crack on Punta Emma. The climb showed him the difference between what he had done so far and what the Devil of the Dolomites could do. Paul did not meet Tita until the next summer, but Punta Emma revealed truths about Tita's character, skills, audacity and aesthetics that mattered more to Paul than anything he could learn in conversation with the man himself.

Roped up to his favourite climbing partner, Paul would have had ample time to consider how Tita felt, unroped, on his own, on terra incognita. Ten years after the first ascent, it was still the hardest climb in the Dolomites. A loose hold, a move that took Tita a few metres onto irreversible ground to a stretch of holdless rock, a strike from even a small falling rock or a slip of the foot in the steep crux chimney crack could have cost him his life. In the comparative backwaters of the Gesäuse, the Totes Gebirge and the other Austrian ranges, Paul was close to the top of the climbing fraternity. But not in the Dolomites.

Climbers impressed by Paul's solo of the Pichl Route, made four years after the Devil of the Dolomites had soloed the first ascent of this much harder route, simply didn't understand how far Tita had taken the game. Despite Paul's later protestations about Tita's use of pitons, Tita's climb on Punta Emma proved to Paul that the ultimate test was not just to solo, climb hard or do new routes. The ultimate test, and the one which he must pass if he was to match what Piaz had already done, was to climb hard, alone, on an unclimbed route.

Tita, seven years older than Paul, became the first man to gain Paul's admiration and respect to the same degree as Eduard had. Tita and Paul had both grown up in the shadow of the Alps; they had both chosen to climb as boys and later forced the climbing world to notice them. Beyond that, though, they were a study in contrasts. Even though Tita was radical, anticlerical, scruffy and indifferent to the law and public approval, Paul – fastidious in his dress, Christian by choice, cosmopolitan and hungry for approval – adopted him as a mentor and almost a father figure.

After Paul's year of finding himself, culminating in his Dolomites debut, he decided to leave Vienna, although he continued to call himself Viennese. The first time he had come to Vienna, as a boy, he had left in a wheelchair, possibly crippled for life; then he had come back to bury his father in the Jewish quarter of the city cemetery. He had come back again on his feet, a Jewish boy with a penchant for truancy in the mountains, fresh out of the provincial *Gymnasium*. He left Vienna in 1910 as a Christian with a university degree and a minor reputation as a mountaineer. Vienna, with its Hausbergen, *Klettergärten*, churches and lecture halls and the ghosts of urbane mountaineers like Purtscheller, the Zsigmondys and Lammer, could offer Paul little more. He had sacked it for all it had to offer a mountaineer. He was off to Munich, the city of climbers.

In Munich, the City of Climbers

Munich was the centre of the climbing world.... The love of climbs both easy and difficult was shared by the royal family, bankers, university professors, writers, army officers and chimney sweeps.
—Aldo Bonacossa

Paul was accepted into the graduate program in plant biology at Ludwig Maximilian University in Munich for the 1910–11 academic year. The university was prestigious, but just as importantly for Paul, Munich, although a quarter of the size of Vienna, was the alpine capital of a country ten times the size of Austria.

Germany embraced modernity. In Munich, there was an impatient urge to let go of the past, to exalt ecstasy and emotion over the type of decadence that fascinated the Viennese. Bavarians glorified youth and renewal. The Jugendstil, or youth style, aesthetic movement began in Munich; its magazine, *Youth*, shared the newsstand with Paul's university climbing buddy Walter Schmidkunz's *German Alpine Times* and *Winter*, along with other mountaineering periodicals published by the numerous local Alpine Club sections. The alpine papers were illustrated by avant-garde painters like Albin Egger-Lienz and climber-artists like Otto Barth, Gustav Jahn, Ernst Platz and Anglo-German painter Edward T. Compton. Beautiful young hikers and climbers of both sexes were favourite subjects, as were *Senners*.

The first generations of mountain enthusiasts to flock to the alpine clubs in the '70s and '80s were getting too old for strenuous days in the mountains. In Austria, a few of the older climbers inspired the new generation with superb memoirs of their days of storm and ecstasy in the Alps. Munich climbers thought more in terms of the future. Bavarian schoolteacher Ernst Enzensperger reacted to the changing demographic of mountaineering by organizing groups to introduce young people to the mountains and train a new generation of "alpine heroes."[93]

The Alps could be seen from Munich. They were part of the familiar landscape, and love of the Alps was no mere daydream for poets and weekend mountain enthusiasts; it was a popular expression of a love of *Heimat*, or homeland. Events and exhibitions with mountain themes sold out. By 1912, 7,580 of the 100,000 members of the German Alpine Club resided in metropolitan Munich. In 1899, the German General Sports Exhibition on Prater Island in the Isar River drew 642,211 visitors, almost 150,000 more people than lived in Munich. One of the most popular attractions was the *Bergsport* exhibit, where sculpture, matte paintings and landscaping recreated the alpine experience.[94]

A visitor offered the following report: "a heavy, threatening boulder... lies loosely over the ravine, we discover an entrance through a rock fissure. We are guided by a cable, such as is used for safety when building paths... and turning around an outcrop, we stand suddenly before one of the grandest high alpine landscapes of the Bavarian Mountains, beneath the Blaue Gumpe in Rainthal, on the path to the Zugspitze. Every visitor is rooted to the spot, spellbound, because they truly believe that they have been transported into one of the grandest mountain landscapes in existence."[95]

The spectacle was repeated with enhancements at the Munich World's Fair in 1898, and a permanent alpine museum with maps and dioramas was opened in 1911. In 1907, the Munich city council donated a handsome building on Prater Island to the Alpine Club for use as a museum. The curator of the museum, judge Karl Müller, called it "an enduring monument to a part of modern cultural endeavour."[96] Munich mayor Wilhelm Georg Ritter von Borscht declared at the opening that the museum was "a monumental pledge to the unbreakable bonds between Munich and the German and Austrian Alpine Club."[97]

Climbers came from across Munich's social spectrum. Tradesmen like carpenter Otto "Rambo" Herzog (whose nickname was adapted from the German term *Ramponieren*, meaning "throwing yourself at a climb") attacked and completed climbing problems with workmanlike zeal. Many doctors, lawyers, academics and even a few members of the upper classes elevated the public profile of the sport and reinforced the authority of climbing clubs. At the Buchenhain *Klettergarten*, climbers who would never meet as equals in the city practised on short climbs up to modern 5.10, a grade not reached at American cliffs until the 1950s.[98]

As a graduate student at the department of botany at Ludwig Maximilian University, Paul moved in a milieu that was at once educated and nationalistic. At the department facilities on the grounds of the Munich Botanical Gardens beside the Nymphenburg Palace, he could study the world-famous collection of specimens its faculty had gathered from the German colonies of German East and West Africa and New Guinea. Austria-Hungary, by comparison, could boast only a single 150-acre colony in Tientsin in China, which was a subject of more levity than pride.

Paul's undergraduate days had been relatively carefree. Life as a graduate student was toilsome. German doctoral degrees were intended for the most talented and single-minded candidates. Not one but two dissertations were required in addition to coursework. Students rarely completed the doctoral degree in fewer than three years. After graduation, they were eligible to be considered for the qualification of *Privatdozent*, or university professor, but that honour was typically withheld for several years. The pace of study would have left few weekends open for climbing, and the oversight of academic advisors made it hard to skip lectures for climbing, as Paul had done so often in Vienna.

Graduate school curtailed Paul's habit of spending every spare moment – and, often enough, moments he should have spent elsewhere – in the mountains. In addition to the demands of his school work, he was short of money. It was a problem compounded by his tendency towards the lifestyle of a *Bummerl* who found activities unrelated to his personal interests hard to sustain. The only job he had held in his life was his short tenure in Zermatt as a language tutor.

He might have become a ski instructor but preferred to give advice for free. He was also ideally suited to the work of a mountain guide. He respected mountain guides, but his embrace of the Viennese ethic of guideless climbing would have made him a hypocrite if he became one himself. Also, with his bourgeois identity, Paul felt it was his calling to have a profession rather than a trade. To remain an amateur was the highest expression of bourgeois love for his vocation as a climber. Circumstance, however, forced him to take a part-time job with a small salary at the Munich Botanical Gardens, which at least was connected to his academic aspirations.

Paul rented a modest apartment on Amalienstrasse in the working-class area of Schwabing, between the university and the parklands of the Englischer Garten. He charmed his Alsatian landlady with the *Alsacien* French accent he had learned from Lina, took long walks in the Englischer Garten and spent much of the last month of 1910 at the nearby Café Stefanie, drinking cheap coffee, playing chess with writers and painters and reading the complementary newspapers.

Climbing trips, when time allowed them, were a financial challenge. In his Vienna years, Paul had travelled at will to any Austrian ranges he liked. His uncle's support, unsupervised undergraduate life, low fees and well-off climbing friends like Relly and Hartwich had contributed to his life as an alpine *Bummerl*.

Luckily for Paul, Munich had local mountains and *Klettergärten*. Paul often cycled the 15 kilometres to the conglomerate rock *Klettergarten* at Buchenhain, where some of the best young rock climbers in Europe practised on problems far harder than what had yet been climbed in the Alps. A typical longer trip for Paul that winter was a stay at the Rotwandhaus, 50 kilometres from the city, in the Mangfall Alps, an area of modest peaks lower than 2000 metres. It was a humble itinerary for a seasoned ski mountaineer. Despite his fastidiousness and distaste for squalor, circumstances had reduced him to a spot on the floor of the *Matratzenlager*, but Paul made the best of it.

One morning, as Paul departed the Rotwandhaus, he saw a couple of novices trying to attach sealskins to their skis. Naturally gregarious and short on German mountain friends, Paul introduced himself and showed them how to use their climbing skins. Walter Bing, one of the young skiers, was impressed by Paul's blue eyes, purple silk necktie and generosity with his time. It turned out that Bing was a law student, a climber and, in an unlikely coincidence, an Alsatian Jew. They both lived in Schwabing and agreed to meet again at Café Stefanie.

Paul and Bing became fast friends and a fixture at the café. Munich secession painter and Café Stefanie habitué Hans Lasser captured them in a double portrait. Paul is in the foreground, gazing at a book, apparently planning an adventure. Bing looks on from the side with a more casual pose, in an obviously junior role. Wearing ties and blazers, they look like a couple of youths inspired by the free alpine newspapers to dream up climbing plans they cannot afford to carry out.

Paul and Bing spent their days off at the Buchenhain *Klettergarten* or hiking in the Englischer Garten. By night, they haunted costume parties like those hosted by Fanny zu Reventlow, the bohemian "Countess of Schwabing." There is no record of Paul's costumes, but it is tempting to imagine him masquerading as one of his departed alpine heroes, perhaps the young Georg Winkler, whose photograph hung on his wall.

A more spartan atmosphere prevailed at the evening meetings of the Alpine Club sections, which were usually held in rented rooms at beer cellars or restaurants. A typical evening's entertainment included club business followed by a talk on a scientific subject or a sombre report on a climb. Witnesses described serious faces, beer steins and clouds of pipe smoke.

Luckily for Paul and Bing, they found the meetings of the Bergland Section more in tune with their bohemian exuberance. Its meetings sometimes ended with drunken feats of buildering, at which, as the section minutes recorded, Paul excelled. What passed as the minutes of one Bergland meeting reads like an account from a student drinking club:

> After the section meeting we went to the Café Maria Theresia in the Augustenstrasse. There, the main attraction was blowing the filling out of cream rolls at each other (the names of the culprits are still known), then we marched to the Königsplatz... A Royal Bavarian

policeman with his pointed helmet saw Doctor Preuss [climbing the Propylaea] and wanted to catch the bastard. Preuss, however, descended the other side of the building, mingled with the passersby and then helped the police search for the climber. In the next carnival season newsletter of the section, the evening was recounted and illustrated with a drawing.[99]

The Propylaea was a neoclassical monument to the Bavarian state's tragicomic attempts to engage in international diplomacy with Greece some 70 years previous. Paul had chimneyed up one of the gaps on the west facade's portico. The climb was sufficiently out of sight of passersby that Paul and Hans Dülfer repeated it often, and no one knew who had climbed it first. When Paul climbed, Bing usually watched for the police, whom Paul referred to as buildering's single objective danger. The lookout was often useless, however, since Paul sang as he climbed and the police came anyway. Throughout his life, Paul showed the city-bound alpinist's proclivity for pranks on buildings, even skiing off the top of a hut in the Insel valley.

In July, Paul and Bing planned a proper climbing trip to the Zugspitze, Germany's highest peak. It was in the Wetterstein Alps near Garmisch-Partenkirchen, less than a 100-kilometre train ride from Munich, but they had to pawn Bing's grandfather's watch to raise the train fare. After the trip, Bing gave Paul 50 marks to redeem the watch, but Paul spent it on a trip to the Dolomites, and the watch stayed at the pawn shop for another year.

In August 1910, on the trip financed by Bing's watch, Paul wrote his uncle Sigmund from the Dreizinnen hut, in the shadow of the high walls of the Tre Cime di Lavaredo. "Having a fairly good time. We climbed seven peaks. I'm famished, the hut is full, I'm low on money, but I'm in a good mood."[100]

Paul was happier penniless and hungry in the mountains than he was settling down to a career in the city. He had started to doubt whether botany was his vocation. Emmy Eisenberg had said that "the love of nature was decisive in [Paul's] choice of profession. You have to love flowers, meadows and woods to study botany."[101] Paul had learned that success in academia, however, depended more on hard work and the sacrifice of climbing time than on the love of flowers and meadows, and he loved mountains more than anything else.

And yet Paul was 24 years old and needed to find a career. His friend Baron Günther von Saar said that when Paul became dissatisfied with biology, he took up empirical philosophy, "intending to become a university lecturer in the near future."[102]

It has also been said that Paul began studies in psychology.[103] It is possible that he learned about that field through Anna and Martin Freud. Early psychoanalysts acknowledged the role of mountains and climbing in what they termed "neuroses." Karl Abraham, for a time Sigmund Freud's chosen successor, shared climbing stories with Sigmund and started work on the definition of an alpine neurosis. "If love of the Alps in general often serves as an outlet for sublimated drives," said Abraham, "this particular form of alpine worship [i.e., bonding emotionally with the mountains] seems to arise from the gratification of a specific complex."[104] Paul would have made a fascinating subject for Abraham's research.

Paul never exaggerated his climbing accomplishments and was sometimes accused of false modesty. His frankness about his own climbing weaknesses (and the weaknesses of other climbers), frustrated his opponents in debates. His claim to the title of doctor is, therefore, a puzzle.

Early writers and Paul's friends and family seemed to have assumed that Paul did the schoolwork and research required for his doctorate. Others maintained that his doctorate was *honoris causa* for his contributions to the field of botany. Records of this degree in the commencements of the university remain undiscovered, and it is hard to see why such a high honour would be awarded to a recently enrolled graduate student with a part-time job at the botanical gardens.

Some biographers mistakenly attributed to Paul the deeds and achievements of his contemporary, the great German plant biologist Paul Rudolph Preuss. Paul Rudolph collected plant specimens in the far-flung German colonies as well as Sierra Leone, Mexico, the Caribbean, South America and Ceylon (now Sri Lanka). Once, in the Cameroons, when the garrison officer of his remote research base was killed, he took his specimens in a backpack and led the garrison to the coast himself. In 1911, he wrote *The Coconut Tree and Its Culture*, the authorship of which is occasionally attributed to Paul Preuss. It is an understandable error, not just because of the shared name but because both men were so intrepid and intelligent, although only one made a career in botany.[105]

Whether Paul used the title to impress people or simply liked the way it sounded, he might have still intended to one day finish the degree that entitled him to it. Neither his family nor friends were troubled by his adoption of the title. Lina, who relied on Paul to eventually take Eduard's place as a provider, may even have taken solace in Paul's hubris.

Freudian psychoanalysis, although now treated with suspicion, was very much a product of the mentality of the 1900s. Would time on Martin Freud's father's famous couch have exposed a system of insecurity behind Paul's self-confidence? Paul was a Jew who had grown up half local and half outsider in traditional, Catholic Altaussee. He proved both his superiority to any who held him in suspicion and his right to the land by climbing above the village in the local mountains. He had been sick as a small boy but survived, although his father had died, giving him at once a sense of his immortality and a bond with his mother by removing the Freudian rival. Had Paul's personal struggle been sublimated into climbing ethics as uncompromising as doctoral studies?

Whether the psychoanalysts would have gotten anywhere with Paul is a moot point, but some said he earned the title of doctor by his written words and dangerous experiments in mountaineering. Their claims may mirror a process in Paul's own mind. In 1911, his academic resolve weakened and he faced the first significant failure of his life. He may have decided that with its high degree of professional excellence, sacrifice and style, his climbing passion earned him a status equal to the bourgeois credentials of a doctor of philosophy. That summer, he would risk his life and alter the course of alpinism in a sudden display of excellence and bravery and show that in climbing, if not in graduate studies, he had few equals.

Allein: Five Days That Changed Climbing, Summer 1911

"What do you see?"
"Not much..."
—exchange between Mina and Paul Preuss during his
reconnoitre of the East Face of the Campanile Basso

As Paul's doubts about an academic career grew, his climbing activity increased. He spent 80 of the 122 days between June 23 and October 23, 1911, in the mountains. Although 39 of these were spent travelling or waiting out bad weather, he made the summits of some 90 peaks, often solo and via previously unclimbed routes. On a trip to the Silvretta range, he made the first ascents of serious new alpine routes on the Southwest Face of the Klein Litzner (2783 metres), the 3122-metre Grosses Seehorn's Northeast Face and the North Face of the Gross Litzner (3109 metres).

Judging from Paul's articles in the *German Alpine Times*, he did not find these routes very challenging. He devoted more words to his friend Edward T. Compton's paintings of the peaks, to jokes about how his watch had altitude sickness and to his musings on the psychology of climbing than he did to the difficulties of the routes themselves. Up until this point, Paul was preoccupied with the inner experience of climbing. He had always spent much of his time on the mountains alone. The rewards he had sought had been personal, from his clandestine ascents as a boy through to his Planspitze solo, which he used as a credential in his applications to exclusive Alpine Club sections but never reported on in detail.

Over five days between July 23 and 29, Paul – previously a sound fellow, quietly respected in the clubs for his special knack for hard climbing and dislike of pitons and rope tricks – made plans that had the predictable result of making him the most noted, or notorious, climber in Europe. In doing so, he set himself on a course of confrontation with the best climbers in the Alps and challenged the meaning and methodology of climbing itself.

So far, no one had so transparently devised to risk everything to become master or martyr of climbing ethics. Even the deaths of the icons of pure alpinism were unpredictable tragedies. The Viennese school's Emil Zsigmondy died when his anchor failed on the Meije in 1885. An avalanche overwhelmed Georg Winkler on the Weisshorn in 1888. Ludwig Purtscheller's fatal pneumonia came months after his 1899 climbing accident on the Dru.

To make his point, Paul would free-solo routes much more difficult than the Dru, the Meije or the Weisshorn. This played to his strengths as a rock climber, to be sure, but it also took his pure ethic into an arena where the use of pitons and rope tension were no longer merely accepted but increasingly seen as essential.

Around 1900, the term *Klettersport* came into use to describe technical rock climbs undertaken not to reach summits but for the difficulty and aesthetic qualities of their rock climbing. *Klettersport* enthusiasts were a new generation of climbers who dreamed more of the high rock walls of the Predigtstuhl, the Totenkirchl and the Fleischbank than the summits of the Matterhorn and Mont Blanc.

Klettersport was defined and popularized by the new techniques and equipment that introduced a degree of safety to rock climbing. Chief among these novelties was the humble karabiner, introduced to climbing in 1911 by Otto Herzog, who had seen the device used on a building site and saw its potential for climbing. Before the karabiner, pitons offered protection that was dubious or hard to use. A rope was laid over a picture-hook piton in the hope that it would snag in the case of a fall. Ring pitons offered more security but required both the leader and follower to untie the climbing rope and thread the rope through the ring, or tie a sling through the ring and around the climbing rope. Karabiners made piton use simple and safer, and as a result, the use of pitons increased. Hans Fiechtl's fixed eyelet piton, designed to accommodate the karabiner, made pitons even more convenient, secure and popular.

Soon, the picture-hook piton became an in situ relic. The rope, the ancient symbol of the communality of the climbing team, and the axe, adapted from the humble farmer's adze and still carried on rock climbs by many climbers, now vied with the heroic leader's hammer.[106]

In 1910, Herzog and Georg Sixt used karabiners for the first time on a strong attempt on the smooth, vertical 800-metre East Face of the Fleischbank. Like many of the peaks in the Kaisergebirge, the Fleischbank, or "meat bank," had a sinister name. Legend had it that a hunter had trapped and then slaughtered a herd of chamois in one of the mountain's gullies. Herzog and Sixt survived their attempt, but the East Face would have to wait for the talented Hans Dülfer. Not to be deterred, in the summer of 1911, Herzog and his sisters, Christina and Paula, used similar techniques to conquer the prominent, beautiful, much discussed North Ridge of the Lalidererspitze.

Another important tool and symbol of *Klettersport* was the *Kletterschuh*. Typical mountain footwear was stiff – ankle-high leather boots with a ring of steel nails around the edges of the sole – but most rock climbers also carried *Kletterschuhe*. Nailed boots offered versatility on talus, muddy paths, icy rocks and less technical ground, but when, as Nieberl said, the rock became so steep and smooth that "it no longer succumbed to the iron-click of your boot nails, the [*Kletterschuh*] allows you to listen to [the rock's] temperamental beauty."[107]

There were two main types of *Kletterschuhe*, both of which had light suede uppers. Felt-soled shoes were less popular and said to be less effective when wet. The most common models had an espadrille sole of thin, plaited rope, similar to those that had been used by alpine shepherds for hundreds of years. There were a few rubber-soled models, but they were viewed with suspicion, and Paul reported that they were slippery.

The *Kletterschuh* held a special place in the hearts and rucksacks of climbers; only the rope had a more vaunted status. Even climbers who stuck to routes with fixed pitons rarely carried hammers, but few climbers in the limestone Alps eschewed the intimacy between feet and rock offered by *Kletterschuhe*. Alpine photographer and writer Guido Rey compared his first experience in *Kletter-schuhe* on the Vajolet Towers to unassisted flight:

> The usual weapon, the axe, was not in our hands; we wore light canvas shoes with soles of twisted rope... the flexible rope soles adhered well to the footholds when they found them, and gripped the smallest granite knobs [Rey elsewhere describes the rock of the Vajolet Towers and the Dolomites more correctly as lime-stone]... the foot adapted itself to the shape of the rock as perfectly as if it had been naked; it felt the solidity of the base which supported it, and freed from all grounds for fear, it stepped confidently on imperceptible ledges that overhung perpendicular cliffs. It was a new experi-ence for me, for this was the first time I had worn the magic shoes; they seemed to me to lend an ideal elas-ticity to the gait, an ideal lightness to the body; and the fear that had at first been instilled into me by the precipitous aspect of the wall gave place to a feeling of confidence and an ecstasy of climbing, as if wings were growing from my feet.[108]

The *Kletterschuh*, much like the pointe shoe introduced into bal-let at the same time, gave weaker participants a chance to try more advanced manoeuvres and created unlimited new possibilities for those who were strong enough to fully exploit the possibilities it created.

Paul invariably wore *Kletterschuhe* on rock. His partners de-scribed a tense magic in the air when the approach was over and Paul upended his rucksack, which usually contained little else be-sides his *Kletterschuhe* on the talus. He sat down, took off his boots, put them in his rucksack and then donned his *Kletterschuhe* with the flourish of a maestro raising his violin to his shoulder.

One of the most famous *Klettersport* athletes was Hans Dül-fer. Often accompanied by his girlfriend, Hanne Franz, Dülfer made first ascents of some 50 new routes, which included some of the hardest climbs in the Alps. Like Paul, Dülfer came from a bourgeois family, had been frail as a boy and was introduced to the mountains by a doting father.

In other ways, Dülfer was very different than Paul. Paul had not inherited his father's talent for the keyboard, but Dülfer was an excellent pianist. Dülfer was unconcerned about his clothes and appearance. He usually wore a threadbare Janker jacket and a workman's cap to cover a head of hair that was so customarily dishevelled it became something of a style statement in itself.

Dülfer was shy and he looked it. He smoked a pipe, as if to avoid being engaged in unexpected conversation. At university, he stayed away from the ubiquitous clubs and parties, and he was awkward when approached with questions about his difficult climbs.

When a star-struck Franz first approached him with a request to be mentored, Dülfer was taken aback and sent her away to get more climbing experience. When she returned shortly afterwards, Dülfer relented and took her on as an apprentice, and then a romantic partner. They moved to the Sparchen neighbourhood in Kufstein, close to the Geisterschmiedwand *Klettergarten*. In an apartment so small that Dülfer's piano had to be moved in through the window, Dülfer and Franz lived in bohemian indifference to the institution of marriage, whereas Paul remained guarded about the nature of his relationships with women, regardless of their propriety.

History remembers Dülfer, somewhat incorrectly, as an enthusiastic proponent of the heavy use of pitons and aid. Dülfer used pitons, sometimes swung across blank sections of rock, and once inspected a route on abseil. He even carried a drill on the Fleischbank, but he never used it. His reputation as a climber who frequently resorted to artificial aid, however, is ahistorical. In 1911, he climbed the Dülferkamin VI (5.9) on the massive West Face of the Totenkirchl, and in 1912, he completed the line Herzog had started on the East Wall of the Fleischbank. Both were predominantly free climbs.

In fact, Dülfer had a sensitive, artistic temperament that made him censorious of an excessive use of climbing technology. He spoke of rock climbing as an aesthetic activity comparable to playing the piano. Paul was less whimsical. "Anyone who wants to tell me," he said, "that in overcoming great technical difficulties, he always thinks of the artwork that nature has created around him I consider childish, or at least an extremely imaginative poet. I'm honest enough to admit that I can forget about the landscape around me on hard climbs and find my pleasure in the purely athletic feelings that produce excellence."[109]

Dülfer once played his keyboard interpretation of Franz Liszt's tense Symphonic Poem no. 1, *Ce qu'on entend sur la montagne*, for Franz Nieberl in his Kufstein apartment. Although Nieberl used the less evocative German name of the piece, *Berg-Symphonie*, the actual title is taken from a Victor Hugo poem, and translates from the French as "what one hears on the mountain." Although Nieberl, a gruff customs officer, claimed not to share Dülfer's good taste in music, Dülfer had chosen the piece wisely. Nieberl claimed that it evoked the fear and awe of being caught out in a storm in his beloved Kaisergebirge.[110]

Dülfer was obsessed with difficulty on both the keyboard and the rock. When he told Nieberl that he wanted to compose an Eroica on the rock, it is more likely that he was referring to Liszt's difficult Transcendental Étude no. 7 in E-flat, "Eroica," for the piano, than to Ludwig von Beethoven's Symphony no. 3 in E-flat Major. Dülfer saw other parallels between music and climbing, and it was said that his climbing style was so refined that he appeared to caress the holds as if they were piano keys.

"It seems strange to me that the majority of climbers know only one urge," he wrote, "which is to go on bagging one summit after another. Are these mountaineers unlike dilettantes on the piano, who superficially, and with no feeling whatsoever, randomly touch the keys as if to play this or that artistic composition without in any way deepening their feeling for the music?"[111]

Although, according to Paul's soon to be heavily publicized philosophies, Dülfer's use of aids technically invalidated his ascents, Paul considered Dülfer a superior rock climber to himself. Dülfer, for his part, considered Paul a master climber.

At first, it looked as if there would always be two separate schools: one that kept to routes that could be done safely without pitons, and another which employed tools and aids on the steep rock that the purists were forced to concede to those willing to use such means. Paul would soon make the climbing world stop and pay attention, sometimes in awe and sometimes in outrage, when he called this division in rock climbing into question and climbed the futuristic lines usually reserved for the piton users without stepping outside of the highest ethical traditions, and thus invented the modern free climb. In doing so, he posed the question of whether pitons and ropes were required on any climbs at all.[112] It was a development that shook the new climbing culture to its core.

He began his tour de force on an objective considered to be the epitome of extreme *Klettersport*, the West Face of the Totenkirchl in the Kaisergebirge – or, as it was known in the local villages, the Koasa. The rugged peaks of this range were famous for their complex natural architecture of canyons, steep ridges and walls of compact, silver-grey Wetterstein limestone. Few of the Kaiser's summits could be reached easily by peak baggers, but it had plenty of potential for rock climbers. Its proximity to Munich made it second in the world only to the Dolomites as a famous stage and laboratory of hard climbing. Young people eager to rock climb flocked to its walls. In 1902, the Kufstein Section of the Alpine Club opened the Stripsenjochhaus, the largest hut in the Eastern Alps, to service the demand for lodgings in the Kaisergebirge. Strips, as it was nicknamed, soon became the home of a new school of climbing, much as Yosemite's Camp 4 would, 50 years later. In the summer of 1911, Adolf Dreye reported that a certain hush fell when Paul sat down at the Stripsenjochhaus dinner table and other climbers tried to steal glances at the dapper, fair-haired prodigy.[113]

Like the Fleischbank, the Totenkirchl, or Chapel of the Dead, had a forbidding name. Its *Führerweg*, or guides' route, however, was relatively simple. The peak only gained an ominous reputation with climbers when they began to explore its long, steep faces of compact, steel-grey rock.

When the summer climbing season of 1911 began, the greatest climb on the Totenkirchl, and one of the hardest routes in the Eastern Alps, was the 600-metre-high West Face, first climbed by

Tita Piaz, Josef Klammer, Rudolf Schietzold and Franz Schroff-enegger in 1908.

Schietzold, who had moved to Munich from the Elbsandsteinge-birge rock climbing region of Saxony, had attempted a bold solo of the wall in 1907, but was turned back after 150 metres. He climbed steep, continuous rock on the right side of the wall. Dülfer and Willy von Redwitz completed Schietzold's project in 1913, after a rappel inspection by Dülfer.

Although Schietzold was a superb climber, he hired Tita to lead his team. Tita, who agreed, later said that Schietzold's offer made the West Wall something "he owed to the future of [his] name." Another perk for Schietzold was that since Tita wasn't officially a guide, Schietzold's climb would earn the prestige of being technic-ally guideless.[114]

Tita, however, lacked confidence in Schietzold's ability alone, and added his friends Josef Klammer and Franz Schroffenegger to the team. He also approached *Kaiserpapst* Franz Nieberl, who was unable to join the climb due to his work.

Guido Rey scoffed that Tita's motorcycle marked him as "a mod-ern."[115] Schietzold had no such qualms and rode the pillion seat on the long journey to the Stripsenjochhaus. The trip would be almost as dangerous as climbing. Tita hit a dog, two chickens and an ox cart loaded with cabbages. He and Schietzold barely escaped unharmed from an altercation with the angry cart drivers.

The next day, Tita inspected the wall with field glasses and chose a line to the left of Schietzold's attempted climb. If his own route didn't go, said Tita, he would live out the rest of his life enclosed in a religious house. After a moment's thought, he added that he meant as the only man in a women's convent.

The climb took about seven and a half hours. Tita led the crux, a slab so smooth that after seconding it, Schietzold said he must have had suction cups on his fingers. The slab was followed by an unprotected overhanging crack that took Tita an hour to climb and offered no protection. Tita had used combined tactics and stood on one of his partners' shoulders to negotiate a steep wall above a belay, a technique still considered within the range of free climbing techniques, but the rest of the climb was free by any standard, and sparsely protected. For a while, it was the hardest climb in the Alps.

After the climb, the team had a photo taken on photography night for the Kufstein Section of the Alpine Club. They sat in a typical alpine-style studio setting with a painted pine tree backdrop and ropes for props. Schietzold smirked and tugged playfully at the bandanna tied in the corners on Schroffenegger's head. Schroffenegger sucked with comic thoughtfulness on a meerschaum pipe. Klammer sat on the floor and stared at Tita with a fixed, adulatory grin. The trio seemed to be purposely aping the kind of goofy *Bergfreunde* who filed up the *Führerweg*. Tita, however, cut a more serious figure. He folded his arms and clenched his hands. His close-cut hair, moustache and Vandyke beard made him look rakish and radical. He scowled at the camera as if he wondered how he had fallen in with his clowning companions.

The picture was published in mountaineering papers along with the report on the climb. Paul and the rest of the climbing public got a chance to meet Tita's fixed outward stare with their own and guess at the depths of sheer will it revealed. Paul would have reflected on his own best achievements, none of which were daring or revolutionary enough to stop the climbing presses. What would it mean to take the next step beyond the West Face of the Totenkirchl?

Paul had climbed hard and usually soloed at a moderate standard on established but not really difficult routes. Tita had soloed hard new routes like the Piaz Crack on Punta Emma. One possible motive for the solos Paul was about to undertake was that he saw Tita as the man to beat. To exceed the standard set by Tita with any certainty, Paul would have to do the West Face of the Totenkirchl in better style than Tita, which meant solo, and also solo a new Dolomites route harder than Punta Emma.

A meticulous person by nature, Paul would have carefully thought out his plan. When he arrived at the Stripsenjochhaus with Walter Schmidkunz and Paul Relly in the third week of July 1911, however, neither of his friends knew of it.

Their first route was the short but difficult North Ridge of the Predigtstuhl.[116] Paul would have had Hans Matejak's solo first ascent of the route in 1908 on his mind as he led, and perhaps even considered it a roped rehearsal for hard solo climbing. Schmidkunz took one of his first action photos of Paul on the crux, the vertical Matejak traverse – a glimpse of Paul's technique of weighting all of the holds equally, even on a vertical wall with small holds. Was he also wondering about the section on the Totenkirchl where Tita had used combined tactics, which he would have to climb unroped and without the aid of a partner's shoulders?

On Sunday, July 23, Schmidkunz and Relly left for Kufstein. If they had known that Paul wanted to solo the West Face of the Totenkirchl, they would have stayed – Schmidkunz to take photos of the hardest solo in the history of the Alps, and Relly in case Paul needed a rescue.

Paul had learned as a boy that loved ones' concern for him impeded his climbing. At the point where soloists' priorities and those of their friends can no longer be reconciled, worries and discouragements first become irrelevant, and then a dangerous distraction.

When Paul stepped out of the hut at ten to five on the morning of July 24, 1911, he avoided all such concerns. His moral universe had a population of one. No one knew his itinerary. Bareheaded and clothed in Altausseer *Tracht*, he blended in with the post-dawn gloom. He carried a whistle in his pocket like the one his father had given him, a rope in case he needed to abseil, some slings, a penknife, and his *Kletterschuhe*, his single concession to climbing technology.

At six o'clock, Paul reached the base of the West Face, which was still in shadow. The compact slabs of Wetterstein limestone and dark overhangs had cowed some of the Alps' strongest climbers. Paul could have turned around at this point and honourably told the story of how he had assessed the climb from below and thought better of it. Instead, he put on his *Kletterschuhe* and began to climb.

No one knew he was there until a party on the way to another route spotted a tiny climber on the West Face. Some gave up their itineraries to watch. Paul had a reputation, and knowledgeable climbers would have easily guessed the name of the madman alone on the wall of the Totenkirchl.

With no need to stop to belay, Paul climbed quickly and confidently up the lower slabs and walls, and paused briefly on the two terraces, where he might have traversed off to easier ground. Paul's ability to climb beautifully, even though he was unroped and hundreds of metres up a wall, inspired Tita to nickname him Lord of the Abyss.[117] Paul earned the title on the Totenkirchl that day, when, instead of following Tita's line at the top of the wall, he continued up a difficult unclimbed crack to a higher finish. Tita's party had taken seven hours. Paul stood on top of his even longer route at 8:45 a.m., less than three hours after he had begun his climb.

In the logbook of the Hinterbärenbad hut, Paul described his variation as "very difficult," and signed the entry "Paul Preuss, Vienna, Bayerland Section – alone." In his route book, he wrote "*allein*" in the margin and underlined it. Like all soloists, he could have avoided the attention and slipped off into the mountains and soloed by and for himself, or at least left his climbs unrecorded. When Paul noted his aloneness in the public hut logbook, however, he drew attention to it, with the rest of the climbing world as his audience. Other climbers' excuses not to do as he had done merely emphasized the genuine, outrageous risks and technical mastery of his pursuits.

Three days later, the newspapers lauded Paul's ascent. Climbing style breakthroughs and controversies usually bored the public, but not this time. To some, Paul was a victorious underdog; to others, he was a superman displaying his powers. Either way, dedicated climbers and uninterested city-dwellers alike knew what it meant to face a challenge alone, as Paul had done.

Partly in response to the attention, Paul admitted that Dülfer, Tita and young climbers like Rudi Redlich were better than him. What set him apart was soloing at the upper end of his abilities, rather than doing the very hardest climbs; those he conceded to talented rivals. His destiny was to show the world how hard he could climb alone.

The Totenkirchl was a remarkable climb, but it turned out to be only a step towards an even harder and more dangerous ascent.

His variant finish on new terrain on the Totenkirchl proved that he was ready to take on the next logical challenge: the solo first ascent of a hard new route.

The Campanile Basso is a 300-metre-high, roughly square-sided pinnacle in the Brenta group in the Dolomites. The Italian name means "low bell-tower": it bears a proportional resemblance to Giotto's 14th-century bell tower, or Campanile, in Florence, but is 100 metres lower than the nearby Campanile Alto. It is steep on all sides, and all routes are sustained and technical. By 1900, the race for the summit of the Campanile Basso had come down to a contest between German and Italian climbers.

Before the collapse of the empire of Austria-Hungary in 1918, irredentism thrived in the Italian provinces of the empire. Italian climbers even founded their own club, the Società degli Alpinisti Tridentini: the Society of Trento Alpinists. In addition to climbing, the club sued German-speaking sections of the Alpine Club that attempted to build huts in Italian-speaking regions.

When, in 1884, German climber Karl Schulz renamed the Campanile the Guglia di Brenta, without even climbing it, the Italians ignored him and stuck with the original name. The first ascent of the tower – and therefore, at least by some traditions, the right to name it – became a matter of national pride. It was such a frightening objective, however, that it was not even attempted until August 1897, ten years after the first ascent of Winkler Tower.

Burning with irredentist pride, Trento climbers Carlo Garbari, Nono Pooli and Antonio Tavernaro made the first attempt, via the line that became the Via Normale. The wine they drank on the ascent emboldened Garbari to advise Pooli to finish the last pitch or die trying, but it was for nought. They retreated 20 metres below the summit. The note they left near their high point, wishing subsequent parties better luck, was written in Italian and presumably not intended for German or Austrian parties. Pooli returned in 1904 and completed his lead, but he was too late for the first ascent.

On August 12, 1899, Austrians Otto Ampferer and Karl Berger attempted the route and found the wine bottles and the note.

They were rebuffed by the same pitch that had turned back Pooli, but returned six days later with a new plan. From the previous high point, they traversed onto easier ground on the North Face to reach the summit. The Italians attributed some of the credit for Ampferer and Berger's to Pooli's route finding, but Nieberl said that Pooli and Garbari had failed due to a lack of *Schneid*.[118]

Tita made the second ascent, on September 26, 1902, with Franz Wenter. Rumours that Tita had planted an Italian flag on the summit, and that it was replaced with an Austrian flag by a subsequent party, fed the international rivalry.[119] In 1908, American Oliver Perry-Smith and German rock expert Rudolf Fehrmann, who had learned to climb on the sandstone towers of Saxony, climbed what became known as the Fehrmann Dihedral on the Southwest side of the Campanile, at IV+ (5.5). The Campanile had been climbed some 80 times by July 1911, most often by the Via Normale, but nationalism continued to tinge the efforts of both sides.

The Campanile's unclimbed East Face epitomized the impossible. The vertical face was not even a last great problem, but something so smooth and relentless that Tita said "even from the base, the route looks like a lie... without cracks, without intermediate resting places, with *noli me tangere* [Jesus's warning to Mary Magdalene not to touch him after his resurrection] firmly engraved on it."[120] No one had even attempted it.

Just four days after his ascent of the West Face of the Totenkirchl, Paul made a speedy trip across Austria to the Dolomites with Relly and Mina. They took the night train from Salzburg to Trento, picked up a car the next morning and drove straight to the Dolomites. At seven o'clock that evening, they arrived at the Bremen Section hut, within reach of the Campanile Basso. On the morning of July 28, 1911, the trio set out, as far as Relly and Mina knew, to climb the Campanile Basso's exciting, but no longer cutting-edge, Via Normale.

The first 200 metres of the climb went quickly. They took a break where the route traversed a long, sloping, rubbly ledge Italian climbers had dubbed the Stadone Provinciale, after the poor-quality local roads. Before they continued on the Via Normale, Paul asked Relly for a belay and traversed around a corner to have a look at the East Face, which rose vertically for 110 metres to the summit.

Relly was surprised that Paul wanted to look at an objective universally considered impossible. But concealed in Paul's jacket pocket was proof that, after his Totenkirchl climb, he had come straight to the Campanile on a secret mission to solo the East Face: a note to leave on the wall to prove his claim. Paul asked for a belay because, unlike on the Totenkirchl, he had his doubts. Relly neglected the belay for a moment to snap a picture of Paul deciding whether or not to solo the first ascent of the East Face.

Paul craned his neck to look for cracks and holds and assess the quality of the rock. First ascents in the Dolomites inevitably involved climbing on uncertain rock. An unroped climber who broke a hold unexpectedly would be lucky to escape a fatal fall. From Paul's position, the wall appeared smooth and ledgeless and the rock quality hard to predict.

"What do you see?" Mina asked.

"Not much," Paul replied.[121]

Not very much was still enough. A few minutes later, Paul took a coiled rope over his shoulder in case he needed to abseil and set out, solo, up the wall. Relly took another photo, which could have been the last photo ever taken of Paul Preuss.

Relly and Mina sat on the ledge and, to take their minds off Paul's dangerous climb, they sang. In this moment – heavy with the impetuosity of youth, the impermanence of life and the beauty of the mountains – they shared their first kiss.

Paul saw none of this as he picked his way up the wall. On the Totenkirchl, he had mainly followed the line taken by the first ascensionists. Here he had to find his own route the whole way. Whenever he felt the route was too difficult, he had to downclimb or traverse; every handhold and foothold had to be tested and each move memorized in case he had to retreat. Every ten metres took him ten minutes to climb, three times what it had taken him to cover the same distance on the Totenkirchl.

The climb pitted Paul's skill and bravery against his mortality, the fragility of his mind, which was never empty when he soloed, and his image of himself as the climber and man who could do this incomparable thing. As long as Paul felt the Campanile bite his fingers and hands as he forced it to carry his weight upwards, he was lord of the void beneath him.

Paul spent two hours on the 110-metre climb, just a half-hour less than he had spent on the 660-metre West Face of the Totenkirchl. The crux of the Totenkirchl, however, was more difficult. In the summit register of the Campanile Basso, he recorded the climb as "difficult and exposed," rather than "very difficult," as he had described the West Face of the Totenkirchl in the Hinterbärenbad hut; later, though, he changed this assessment to "extremely" difficult.[122]

Eighty of the best climbers in Europe had written their names in the summit register of the Campanile Basso, and none had recorded an effort as proud as Paul's. Even if he had compromised his principles and abseiled, his solo was the best climb in the range in several seasons, and the best ever solo climb. But Paul had one more statement to make that day. Showing a breathtaking commitment to his ethics, he downclimbed rather than abseiled.

He rejoined Relly and Mina and continued with them up the Via Normale to the summit for the second time that day. Relly photographed Mina in a broad-brimmed hat, climbing up a ridge to a ledge where Paul stood, casually belaying her. Even after soloing the hardest route in the Dolomites, Paul looked relaxed and natural in his role as the senior amateur climber. A couple of days later, Relly and Paul climbed the Fehrmann Dihedral on the Campanile, and after the Fehrmann route, he downclimbed the East Face solo, making for three ascents and two downclimbs of the Campanile in three days.

The route was finally repeated in 1924, by Karl Aichner, Franz Bernardi and H. Buratti. In 1927, it acquired an ominous reputation when broken holds sent Italian climber Pino Prati and his partner Giuseppe Bianchi to their deaths. It was not soloed again until 1936, by Italian ace Emilio Comici.

The reaction to Paul's climb was immediate. The style was so daring and original that it transcended nationalism. Italian climber Angelo Dibona, who made the first ascent of the massive North Face of the Lalidererspitze with pitons that summer, admitted that "although [the East Face of the Campanile Basso] is short, it's the way of the future in the Dolomites." Tita was as impressed by Paul's style as he was by the difficulty of the route. "And for this wall," he said, "Preuss is ropeless, without any security, and even descends it!"[123]

Paul continued with a spate of difficult new routes. On August 1, on the Crozzon di Brenta, Paul and Relly made the first ascent of the 800-metre Northeast Wall in just five hours. Paul's reputation grew with every climb he did, and Schmidkunz saw a scoop in his friend's sudden notoriety. He accompanied Paul on the first ascent of the Southwest Face of the Grohmannspitze via the chimney now known as the Preusskamin. Around this time, they began to discuss an article in which Paul would write out the principles behind his climbs, to be published in the August issue of Schmidkunz's *German Alpine Times*.

In late August, Paul and Relly made the first ascent of a difficult 250-metre crack on the southeast corner of the Cima Piccolissima of the Tre Cime di Lavaredo (Drei Zinnen). The so-called Preussriss, or Preuss Crack, became one of the most feared climbs in the Alps and was later the scene of six fatal accidents.

Before Paul left the Dolomites for Altaussee, he finally met Tita in person. They spent a day enchaining routes on the Vajolet Towers, and despite their differences in climbing style, they quickly developed a tense but sincere friendship. At dinner in the Vajolet hut that night, they drained bottles of wine with the climbers staying there. When everyone was drunk, some climbers teased Tita with overly fulsome praise for his climbs. Severino Casara imagined how the conversation would have gone:

> "Stop," said Tita. "I know who the best climber is, it's him [Paul]. He is better than everyone. Now don't curse and deny it. In front of this man, I feel like a pygmy!"
>
> Tita rhymed off Paul's climbs in detail, finishing with the Totenkirchl West Face and the East Face of the Campanile Basso. Paul pointed to the Punta Emma in response.
>
> "You climbed that solo and made new routes on the

Vajolet Towers when I was just a boy, and just the other day, another new route on the Delago Tower."

"You can't argue with me," said Tita, "you climb without a rope, always free, with no backup, like you did today. I was biting my nails."

"But you are the Devil of the Dolomites," said Paul. "I am just a poor novice."

"You climb better than me!" Tita insisted. "That's the truth!"

Paul disagreed, and Tita stormed into the hut and came back with a brace of old pistols. He handed one to Paul and took ten paces backwards. The gathered climbers stopped talking. Unlike Martin Freud and many Jewish students in Catholic Vienna, Paul had avoided duels up until this point. Nonetheless, he took a pistol, tucked one arm behind his back and aimed the gun at Tita's chest.

"Now, tell me who is the better climber, or shoot!" shouted Tita.

Schmidkunz, who already knew that Paul had a manifesto in the works in which he would establish himself as a rival to Tita, grabbed his camera. His photo of the two men pointing pistols at each other was the second snapshot taken of Paul that summer that might have become the last photo of him alive. Tita's placid Bernese, Satana, sat in the background, indifferent to his master's antics. The mood was broken by the pop of a wine bottle cork. The duellists declared themselves satisfied, embraced and went back to their cups, although later that night, a new argument was kindled over the use of pitons and ropes.[124]

Despite their differences in class, age and education, there was a natural bond between Paul and Tita. Tita felt a mixture of appreciation of Paul's skills, fear for Paul's life and concern about his hubris. Even on that first night, Tita suspected that beneath Paul's self-effacing claims lay a dangerous ambition.

The Totenkirchl and the Campanile Basso, climbed solo in quick succession, had shown that Paul's priorities differed from those of most climbers. Paul's credo would soon be discussed by almost every climber in Europe. For now, all who knew his climbs agreed that he was the first to live by an ideal that made tricks with ropes and pitons look tawdry, even when their use was a matter of life and death. Tita, a man of the world, saw right away that Paul's climbing was fine and true but that his new project of converting climbers to his point of view could end badly.

That summer, Paul's ethics hardened. He wanted to eschew pitons and rope tension not just because it was better to climb without them but because these elements were, existentially, alien to real alpinism. Now he fretted when he attached his rope to in situ protection pitons on the Rizzikamin on the Innerkoflerturm, even though the deep crack was notoriously wet, awkward and mossy in places. The act had turned his attempt on the Rizzikamin into a non-climb.

In early September, Paul visited his family in Altaussee before he returned to Munich. As usual, he hoped to get in some climbing, so when Mina asked him to join her on the Trisselwand with her friend Grete Loew and Loew's guide, Hans Hüdl, Paul readily agreed.

Loew climbed slowly, and it was late afternoon by the time they reached the exit pitches. Paul made a traverse on poor rock that exposed the less experienced climbers to the possibility of a long, unprotected fall. By the time the two novices could be coached safely across the traverse, it would be dark. Paul had made many unplanned bivouacs, beginning when he was a boy on his first serious climb on the nearby Bischofsmütze. Hüdl, however, worried about how his client would weather a night in the rough. Paul looked for an alternative route, climbing with the deliberate, slow style developed over years of climbing without protection. Hüdl finally lost his patience.

"Place a piton!" shouted Hüdl.[125]

Paul descended to the rest of the party but was unsure of what to do next. Hüdl took a hammer and some pitons out of his rucksack. Paul looked at Loew, who shivered from cold and fear at the prospect of an open bivouac. Paul looked at the pitons and hammer in Hüdl's hands. He had risked his life and reputation to prove the hardware unnecessary, and the issue of the *German Alpine Times* containing his anti-piton manifesto had just hit the newsstands. He had used in situ pitons on the Rizzikamin. Placing pitons himself would be a step further away from his ethics. Once Loew had seen the expedient to escape nightfall, however, Paul could not easily turn it down in front of her.

"As much as I abhorred such means," Paul wrote, "I had to resign myself to using them. But using [pitons] is not so easy and I only managed to place two with great difficulty. With their assurance, I made the traverse safe."[126] Paul had not used such emotional language about pitons before. Hüdl had only done his job by coming prepared for an emergency with the pitons, but he had annoyed Paul nonetheless.

According to tradition, these were the only pitons Paul ever placed. In the 1970s, Emmy Eisenberg gave Reinhold Messner a crude picture-hook piton and a hammer she said had belonged to Paul. Both items are now on display at the Messner Mountain Museum Corones on the Kronplatz. It is probable, however, that Hüdl left the pitons on the Trisselwand to use the next time he guided the route; the time and effort required to remove them would have defeated the purpose of using them in the first place.

The summer of 1911 will always be remembered as the one in which Paul became a hero of climbing style, but it ended with proof that the hardest climbing rules were provisional. In the *Styrian Alpine Post*, Paul said he had compromised out of concern for the women in the party. Paul enjoyed the company of women, but his willingness to blame his choice on them, rather seeing it as the best option for the whole party, betrayed a merciless devotion to his climbing philosophies. To Paul, Grete Loew's fear of an open bivouac, of the kind he had survived numerous times, was irrational. "Women do not know fear," he wrote, "only [irrational] terror."[127]

The experience deepened Paul's animus towards pitons and the climbers who used them. Later, when Paul heard a couple of pitons jangle in Walter Schmidkunz's pockets, they reminded him of this incident, and Paul asked Schmidkunz to at least pack them separately where he could not hear them.

Paul now lived to embody his ideals with as few compromises as possible. He removed fixed ropes that had been left in place on popular routes to expedite faster, safer ascents or retreats. He might also have removed pitons, but that would have meant the inconvenience of carrying a hammer, and soft steel pegs were hard to remove. He started to publicly confess his infractions against his ideals. From then on, he rarely backed off climbs, even in bad weather.

Paul tried to bring the world into line with his ideals, which is the goal of a fanatic, but continued to present himself as a well-dressed bourgeois gentleman with fine manners. He spread his alpine gospel not through pamphlets, like a revolutionary, but in print periodicals, with their learned mystique, and the evening lecture, with its redolence of the men's club.

Paul discovered that his actions and words fed upon each other. The more he talked about his ideas, the more he lived them out on hard climbs that, in turn, justified further words on his philosophies. There was a duality at the heart of his being.

The existentially pure climber who had first proved himself alone against the mountains as a Jewish boy disguised as a *Senner*; and the created, bourgeois, Christian fellow he was in the city – these were personae born of his internal crisis of self-identity and worth. One for his dreams, the other for his nightmares; one for action, one for reflection; one for disguise, one for revelation. Now he forced a crisis through which these two identities fused. In thought, word and deed – with some struggle, embarrassment and, finally, triumph – he recreated himself.

A Crazy Notion: The Great Dispute, 1911–12

I stand just about alone in my opinions, and whenever I expressed something of them, the answer was always: "Quite an ideal point of view, but a crazy notion."

—Paul Preuss

Climbers who picked up the August 1, 1911, issue of the *German Alpine Times* at the newsstand expected the usual articles reporting on trips and climbs, illustrated with grainy reproductions of aquatint landscapes. Instead, the lead article leapt from the pages in bold script, framing a photo plate of a stone bust of Ludwig Purtscheller, who stared at them blankly, as if from the afterworld.

With his academic career in limbo, a wild climbing season still underway and a bank account in decline, Paul had penned his first piece, one of the most explosive, idiosyncratic, anachronistic and yet perennially relevant documents in the history of climbing: "Artificial Aids on Alpine Routes." It was the first of more than 30 pieces Paul wrote between 1911 and 1913. A few appeared in the newsletters and journals of the German and Austrian Alpine Club and in touring magazines, but most were published in one of Schmidkunz's three titles, the *German Alpine Times*, the hunting magazine *The Chase* and the ski magazine *Winter*.

After university in Vienna, Schmidkunz had moved to Munich, where he worked for the publishers of the *German Alpine Times* as a writer, editor and photographer. He founded his own publishing house, and in 1913, he acquired rights to numerous climbing titles and the perennial bestseller *Climbing Rock* by Franz Nieberl.[128]

Schmidkunz knew what his public wanted and was up to date on the latest trends, from hand-held cameras to style wars in climbing. Climbers loved print media. The 700-page annual journal and associated publications of the German and Austrian Alpine Club cost over half of the club's annual revenues. The sections produced and financed their own newsletters and reports. Commercial newsstand papers and journals such as the *Alpine Friend*, the *Alpine Monthly Notebook* and Schmidkunz's titles filled in the gap between these publications.[129] The demand for magazines and the competition for the eyes and money of climbers was high.[130]

Paul and Schmidkunz both belonged to the Munich Academic and the Bayerland Sections. In 1911, the year Paul did his big solos on the Totenkirchl and the Campanile Basso, Schmidkunz climbed with Paul, photographed him and commissioned "Artificial Aids on Alpine Routes."

There had been imbroglios in the mountain community before, but this was different. Paul wrote about the soul of climbing and called out those who he believed threatened it. Schmidkunz hoped that if he handled Paul's article properly, climbers across Germany would buy the *German Alpine Times* just because of its controversial content, leaving the *Alpine Friend* and the *Alpine Monthly Notebook* on the shelves. Schmidkunz also knew that Paul could use the writer's fees.

The end of the 1911 climbing season left Paul in a vulnerable position. Relly apprenticed at a legal firm; Hartwich and Bing enrolled in medical residencies; Schmidkunz had his publishing company; Martin Freud volunteered for the Imperial Horse Artillery; other university friends moved on to their adult careers. Paul, despite his climbing success, doubted that biology was the right subject for him. Writing gave him a task with bourgeois cachet and supplied him with a small but much-needed income.

Schmidkunz had a manifesto on his hands and knew it. He had already switched most of his content from traditional Fraktur script to the Latin alphabet, but he typeset Paul's article in old-fashioned Fraktur. Photos of the Totenkirchl or Relly's snap of Paul solo on the Campanile Basso would have reminded the readers of the author's credentials. Instead, Schmidkunz linked Paul to one of the great lights of modern mountaineering with the photograph of the Purtscheller bust – as if Paul's words might as well have come from the mouth of the father of guideless climbing.

The article was the first salvo in a debate about rock climbing style that would rage for decades. Personalities from throughout the climbing world joined the dispute, which would come to define the issues at the heart of climbing.

"Artificial Aids on Alpine Routes," is short but complex. Its philosophy still has interest and relevance, but terms like "sport climbing," "artificial aids," "modernity" and even "rock climbing" itself carried different and sometimes even opposite meanings to what they would a century later. The entire dispute can only truly be understood in its historical context.

Paul began with the observation that he had no followers and that most people would believe his philosophy to be "quite a crazy notion." Reasonably enough, however, he excluded from his critique the use of cables, rails, stairs and other aids for beginners and hikers. He promised to focus his critique on technical mountaineering and rock climbing.

The goal of rock climbing, he said, was to ascend a certain facet of a mountain, such as a wall, pillar or ridge, for its own sake, rather than to reach the summit. The measure of a rock climb's worth, or its sport value, derived principally from its difficulty, although the beauty of the line taken by the climb played a role. An alpine climb, on the other hand, derived its beauty principally from the line taken to the summit of a peak, and difficulty was less important.[131] Mountaineering and rock climbing had different objectives, but they shared rules and the spirit of true sport.

For Paul and other alpinists of the 1900s, to climb sportingly was to measure one's abilities against the mountain. Josef Ittlinger summed it up:

> Man has the standard in himself for his own achievement, which only he is capable of evaluating. Only when he compares his achievements to those of other people does competition arise. We do not regard the struggle against inanimate objects like mountains as a competition, nor measuring strength against others. In the soul of man dwells an ineradicable strong instinct to use his mental

and physical powers to measure difficult and dangerous tasks. It has a special attraction to him to see how far his powers will take him and to judge their quality on the basis of his achievements. The greater and more perfect that achievement, the greater his powers and the greater his satisfaction, and, in certain circumstances, this satisfaction can even lead to ecstasy. The rules of sport do not have to serve only competition [between climbers].[132]

To Paul, artificial aids, specifically the use of pitons and rope tension, even on descents, negated the sports value of any climb. Abseiling was already avoided because of the risk of anchor or rope failure and because it was seen as good practice to abseil only when necessary. Paul said that abseils should be eschewed not because of these reasons but because they constituted aid. Free climbing was the single valid means of ascent or descent. Abseiling might be used as an emergency measure, but even then, it invalidated an ascent. "If you cannot climb down," Paul said, "you should not climb up."[133]

A traverse was not to be claimed if the climbers abseiled any part of it. Both of Paul's examples of traverses, the Vajolet Towers and the Campanile di Val Montanaia, were – not coincidentally – first claimed by Tita Piaz, who abseiled on the descents. Paul also called out Tita for his Tyrolean traverse to the summit of the Guglia Edmondo De Amicis even though he knew Tita did not consider the ascent valid. He could have set that climb against Tita's great ascents like Punta Emma, but he did not. Whether or not Paul wrote these criticisms of Tita before he met him that summer, they show a desire to engage him in a dispute. Paul admired and respected Tita. Although he had been conciliatory and respectful towards Tita when he had met him, Paul now rebelled against him like a teenage boy acting out against his father, a stage of individuation that Eduard's death had denied Paul.

Paul also criticized the use of what he saw as excessive protection. "The thought: 'if you fall, you'll hang three metres on the rope [from a piton]' is of lesser ethical worth than the feeling: 'one fall, and you're dead!'"[134] He characterized well-protected climbing as mere "gymnastics on steep walls with absolute security," and therefore a bad practice.

For Paul, any route that could not be climbed as if the rope was not there should be "left alone immediately." Once a climb was left alone, the issue of its safety was irrelevant because it endangered no climbers.

If, Paul said, protection was so poor that a fall by either member of a roped party would drag both climbers to their death, the partnership was undermined by a subconscious (*unterbewusstsein*) urge towards self-preservation. Under such circumstances, only one climber should tie in, and the other should only try to hold a fall as long as he could before being pulled off. He thus put limits on the traditional fellowship of the rope.

Paul rejected the use of the piton so vehemently that the dispute he started became known as the Mauerhakenstreit, or the Piton Controversy. Metal climbing aids driven into stone walls had been used for thousands of years, and yet their status in climbing had been disputed since climbing had become a sport, in the 19th century. "Now comes a piece of equipment," said Franz Nieberl, "which has given rise to both nonsense and glory, namely, the piton."[135] Nieberl wrote in 1909, just before the karabiner and Fiechtl's eyelet piton made pitons more secure and numerous. Paul complained of 22 pitons on a single climb, enough in his opinion to eliminate the need for safe lead climbing and route finding.

Many climbers, however, thought that judiciously placed pitons, as long as they were not used as hand or footholds, enhanced rather than destroyed their experience. Paul believed that the piton exerted a sinister fascination that defeated any impulse to moderation. Like a preacher trying to win over a sinner, he confessed that he had "wanted" to overcome climbs with pockets full of pitons before he had seen that abuse was the inevitable outcome of the use of even a single piton.

Paul said that even when climbing with pitons, the safety of the rope was sometimes an illusion. His solution to the problem was simplistic and reductive. Climbers should not attempt climbs from which they might fall. The problem was that most falls were unexpected, and even an advanced climber could make a mistake. To climb hard, was, by definition, to risk a fall.

The article was still on the newsstands when Paul compromised the principles contained therein and placed two pitons on the Trisselwand. He later blamed his climbing partners for this peccadillo, but it showed that on the mountain, he answered to the needs of his partners as well as his philosophies. In the conclusion of his article, he briefly feinted at compromise and said that he was not levelling "unfulfillable demands," but "a few suggestions" which he conceded would be dismissed as "extreme" or "hypermodern." In his last sentence, however, he resumed his firmer stance. "I believe myself to be carrying out a return to the declining alpinism of the purest style," he wrote, "to the alpinism on whose solid ground and soil I believe myself to be standing, body and soul."[136]

Paul had already struck a religious tone when he called climbing a chivalrous battle against the mountain. To conclude, he adapted the famous words spoken by Martin Luther, the founder of the denomination of his adoptive religion, at the Diet of Worms in 1521. When Luther was asked if he would recant the contents of his Protestant books, he took some time to pray, returned and stated that all he could do was to remain faithful to the truth, even if accused of heresy. "*Hier stehe ich, ich kann nicht anders* – Here I stand, I cannot do otherwise." Few Germans did not know those words.

Schmidkunz was ecstatic. Paul's article made for his bestselling issue of the *German Alpine Times*. Hans Dülfer reported that even months after the article was published, climbers in Munich were still talking about it.[137]

Tita was surprised and upset by the piece. Schmidkunz, who wanted to keep the debate and sales alive, asked him to respond in writing. Tita had already been asked to respond to Paul on behalf of unnamed climbers opposed to Paul's self-described "hypermodern" views.

Reinhold Messner has observed that Paul had not asked the climbing community to do any more than he had done.[138] He was 25 years old, and on more than 1,000 climbs he had stuck to his principles on all but a few occasions. He had never had an accident. He had never sacrificed a companion's safety. He had made a plea for a style-driven alpinism that, in his eyes, proceeded directly from the nature of the activity, but this natural approach had not been given a fair attempt in the rush to employ pitons and rope work.

Messner was more sympathetic than Paul's contemporaries. Tita had already acknowledged that Paul was the best climber, and now, with characteristic egalitarian feeling, Tita said that he would embrace Paul's views when 51 per cent of climbers were as good as Paul. Tita's essay was simply entitled "Artificial Aids on Alpine Routes, A Response."[139]

To begin, Tita clarified that he was "talking about pitons as a means of protection, not as ladder rungs; for [I] too find climbs characterized by a huge number of pitons to be at the very least ridiculous."[140]

Tita was seven years older than Paul and had daughters and a wife, and this life experience showed in his words. "We were men before we became climbers," he said. "The climber must not repress the man... our relatives have more right to us than the most shining of climbing ideals. Had the most ridiculous use of pitons saved a single human life, its use would already have been justified thereby."[141]

Paul's dictum that it was better to risk death than mere injury scandalized Tita. "In the event of a fall," Tita said, "it is better to hang four or even twenty metres on a protective rope (perhaps with a broken leg) than have the ravens celebrate a feast with our corpse in the dark abyss."[142]

Tita agreed that abseils should be minimized, but downclimbing on difficult rock like the Vajolet Towers invited tragedy. "On a ticklish retreat down a vertical face," Tita warned, "the slightest circumstance is apt to cause a catastrophe!"[143]

Tita dismissed Paul's comparison of climbing to a battle in which both the mountain and the climber were equally armed. Tita compared the mountain to an unfairly well-armed, aggressive and powerful enemy against which puny climbers were no match, even with artificial aids. Truly chivalrous climbers protected themselves and their partners by climbing safely.

Tita accused Paul of endangering professional guides who were in the mountains for work, not thrills. For guides, said Tita, "wherever danger threatens, the use of pitons is of the strictest moral duty."[144]

Paul had ended by evoking Martin Luther. The anarchist Tita concluded with praise for alpine freedom: "I do not at all understand how a person can be so cruel as to want to constrain rock-climbing within limits; after all, we go into the mountains to be free of limits! We go into the mountains to steer clear of all constraints, not to stumble over an even more dangerous one."[145]

Schmidkunz's battle now had two sides. Both Paul's admirers and his detractors would buy the climbing papers to follow their champions. Schmidkunz decided to run Tita's article and Paul's reply side by side in October.

Paul's surprise at Tita's umbrage betrays his immaturity and his unrecognized need to define himself over and against a male role model he actually admired. He called Tita's response "scathing," even though Tita had balanced his criticism with compliments. Paul's real problem, claimed Tita, was an excess of climbing talent and a lack of life experience.

Paul began his counter-response with the admission that his ideas "have gone somewhat too far for practical application."[146] Paul's words lacked compassion. "We were men before we became climbers, that is true," Paul said. "We want to prove it by allowing thoughts to prevail over feeling, the mind to hold sway over body."[147] He criticized Tita for comparing climbing to a battle, even though he himself had done so in his own article.

Paul was at times unreasonable. "How many falls tell of poorly driven pitons," he asked; "how many fatalities has poor abseiling already cost?"[148] Paul observed that although Tita, along with most climbers, condemned the placement of pitons as handholds, they had nonetheless proliferated to the point where even their use as protection constituted an abuse. The only solution was to ban them altogether.

Novices, Paul said, should be taught to climb without technological backups like pitons and abseils. Fixed abseil ropes should be removed. He boasted that he had removed 60 metres of fixed abseil rope from the Southeast Ridge of the Totenkirchl; 80 metres from the Schmittrinne, a variation on the *Führerweg* on the Totenkirchl; and 90 metres from the North Face of the Hochtor.

Paul countered Tita's anarchist coda with a reification of climbing values: "I am not the one who wants to force rock-climbing into limits! It has itself set these limits; they lie in the concept of sport, which we can no longer change... should I not uphold the highest principle of sport – and, so far as I can, also hold back others to that end – the principle that is common to every sport and ennobles every sport, the principle of purity of style? Beautiful climbing, in a technological as well as an ideal respect, means good climbing, and good climbing means secure climbing!"

Paul proposed to establish safety by banning safety measures, to force climbers to take ultimate risks to teach them never to take ultimate risks, to remove every safety aid to serve a higher conception of safety, to put climbers in harm's way to teach them to climb securely. His only exception was for guides, whose climbs had less sporting value than those of amateurs.

The longest, most withering and personal response to Paul's original article came on November 30 from Franz Nieberl, published not in the commercial alpine papers, which Nieberl held in disdain, but the *News of the German and Austrian Alpine Club*. Nieberl began by likening the controversy to a destructive thunderstorm and a fire that must be checked lest it burn down the house of alpinism. The storm had, in Nieberl's words, brought forth "a seemingly sweet but all the more poisonous fruit."[149]

Ugly innuendoes in Nieberl's response alluded both to Paul's Jewish descent and his Protestant conversion. He compared Paul's call to action to the anti-Catholic "Away from Rome!" movement and calls Paul "the newly arisen Puritan of rock climbing." Here, to cast doubts on Paul's Austrian patriotism, Nieberl alluded to the rumour that German Protestant alpinists had secret nationalist and missionary intentions in the mountains.[150]

Nieberl also took on Paul's ancestry. He accused Paul of spreading "false doctrines" and called him a "terrible Moloch." In the Old Testament books of Leviticus, Jeremiah and 2 Kings, pagans burned their infant children alive as sacrifices to the god Moloch. Austrian anti-Semites used Moloch as a symbol of Judaism.[151]

Nieberl said that Paul represented "a decadence of rock climbing... an extra-high tension, almost perverse titillation of the senses for the exhausted nervous system that no longer reacts to gentler stimuli." Those who followed Paul "on his bold, sportingly conducted rock-climbing path" would end in destruction.[152] Paul would realize his folly too late, like Goethe's sorcerer's apprentice.[153] Nieberl condemned as a "bacillus" the urge to turn climbing into a sport with death as a possible acceptable outcome. Paul was a vector of the disease, a "sports-alpinist and only a sports-alpinist of the purest stamp." Judaism, not incidentally, was often described in similar biological terms by contemporary German-speaking anti-Semites.[154]

Mixed in with Nieberl's ad hominem remarks were more-solid points. Chief among these was his reminder that "aid" was a subjective term. Paul accepted climbing boots, ice axe and rope as legitimate gear, but classified pitons as illegitimate aids. But most climbers believed that pitons were legitimate, and their opinion should not be discounted.

Like Paul, Nieberl disliked unnecessary abseils and fixed abseil ropes, tight ropes that turned second climbers into "human sacks of potatoes"; he also disapproved of claiming summits of pinnacles by Tyrolean traverses. He rejected the use of pitons as holds, or even their use in quantity as protection. "I would not like to do routes either under the aegis of the [piton-enthusiast] Laliderer Wall climbers or under that of Preuss,"[155] he said. The Laliderer comment referred to a hard 900-metre, ten-piton route on the Lalidererspitze completed the previous summer by Angelo Dibona, Luigi Rizzi and Guido and Max Mayer.[156]

Paul was horrified by these images of himself as a vector of disease, a Moloch, a Puritan, a mere sportsman and an apprentice playing with powers beyond his control while leading hapless followers to their doom. His response in the December 15 issue of the *News of the German and Austrian Alpine Club* was called "Artificial Aids on Alpine Routes: A Reply by Paul Preuss in Vienna."

Paul wanted the readers to know right away that he was Viennese like Purtscheller, and an Austrian like Nieberl.

Paul lamented that his ideas "are not judged so tragically by my friend Piaz." Readers of Nieberl's article, Paul said, "likely take me for a really wild and unbridled companion, for whom nothing, not the lives of strangers only but not even his own life, is sacred.[157]

"It was immensely regrettable," said Paul, "that Herr Nieberl was incapable of separating the subject matter from the person and permitted himself to be led in his way of regarding theoretical opinions by a prejudice toward my person. Yet, however much he may take me for the pure, incorrigible sportsman capable of none but sporting feelings, I still don't believe that a refutation of this view, or the view itself, falls within the scope of a public discussion of theoretical questions."[158]

Unlike some of Paul's earlier, bruised responses to criticism of his ideas about climbing, there was something dignified and even practised in this retort to Nieberl's veiled anti-Semitism. Unlike his insecure objections to Tita, it was pure polemic. Nieberl's tone galvanized Paul to clarify his thinking, moderate his position and make a succinct, relevant and rhetorically sound statement on climbing style.

Rock climbing, Paul said, was a separate activity from mountaineering by definition of the Alpine Club. His proof was that a climb of the Totenkirchl by the easy route qualified to be recorded in the Alpine Club's annual climbs report because the summit was 1500 metres above sea level. He cheekily referred to Nieberl's difficult Nieberlkamin route on the same peak as an example of a pure rock climb that was much more difficult than a mere ascent to the summit via the easiest route, yet did not qualify as a mountaineering ascent because it ended below that 1500-metre mark.

"Rock climbing and skiing are perfectly capable of existing by themselves [i.e., apart from mountaineering]," Paul said.[159] He wanted the two sports to thrive alongside each other in pursuit of separate but related goals.

He avoided strictly defining where aids begin and end, although he later remarked sarcastically that when "my fingertips were climbed through, adhesive tape had to come to my aid, which even the severe critic probably won't charge as a violation of my theories on artificial aid since I used the adhesive tape with the sticky side facing inward."[160]

Paul distilled his views into principles which he referred to as "theses," after the style of the famous Ninety-Five Theses that Martin Luther nailed to church door in Wittenberg in 1517. It was another loan from his own religion, and a well-known heroic moment in German history. His theses, like Luther's, were short and pithy:

1. You should not be equal to the mountain climbs you undertake, you should be superior.

2. The degree of difficulty that a climber is able to overcome with security on the descent and also believes himself capable of with an easy conscience must represent the upper limit of what he climbs on the ascent.

3. The justification for the use of artificial aids consequently only arises in the event of an immediately threatening danger.

4. The piton is an emergency reserve and not the basis for a method of working. The rope is permitted as a relief-bringing means but ought never be the one true means for making the ascent of the mountain possible.

And what I gladly concede:

5. The principle of security ranks among the highest principles. But not the frantic correction of one's own insecurity attained by means of artificial aids, rather that primary security which with every climber should be based in the correct estimation of his ability in relation to his desire.[161]

Paul also said that he accepted the use of pitons as a last resort in emergencies.[162] He rejected the Saxon climbers' limited use of ring pegs hammered into holes for aid to complete climbs.[163] He agreed with Saxon experts like Rudolf Fehrmann, however, that self-assurance is more important than protection."[164]

Paul had come off as unconvincing and fanatical in his first article. Now he said that if climbers gave up the "craft-like pursuit" of climbing with ropes and pitons for a new pursuit judged and regulated according to free climbing style, the "intellectual and mental education of a mountaineer" would mean that although "now, the mountains are hated, fought and waged war against by every means, we shall learn once more to fear and to love [*fürchten und lieben*] them!"[165]

As if committing his theses to the canon of history, Paul closed by echoing the words of a great German prophet: Luther's "*fürchten und lieben*." The exchange marked a turning point in Paul's favour, not just in the Piton Controversy but in the history of climbing, and raises the question of whether modern free climbing was defined in response to an anti-Semitic slur.

Paul now presented a philosophy of climbing at once sporting in its rules, romantic in its view that a basic, unfiltered experience of the mountain is desirable and possible, existential in that it proposed giving up hollow achievements for ideals, and practical in that it translated these concepts into real climbing situations.

Fearing he was losing control of the controversy he had launched, Schmidkunz solicited Paul Jacobi, a 26-year-old acquaintance of Paul's, to write an objection to Paul in the form of the somewhat patronizingly named "Marginal Notes" in the *German Alpine Times* in November.[166] Jacobi warned readers not to credit Paul's ideas simply because of "the popularity that the name [Preuss] enjoys (despite or because of the youth of its bearer)."[167] By contrast, Jacobi said that Nieberl had "an opinion that stands contrary to Preuss's. And yet Preuss will hardly succeed in branding a man like Nieberl as an outdated authority."[168]

Jacobi pointed out that Paul did not distinguish between emergency and excessive use of aids. Instead of pursuing this point, however, Jacobi inadvertently made one of Paul's points for him when he inferred that according to the strictest application of the theses, "pretty much our entire active development in the Alps, will, from the alpine and rock-climbing point of view, probably be absolutely worthless." The complaint had already been voiced by Tita, but they both exaggerated the threat to history.[169] Few of the first ascents of the golden age of alpinism had involved significant aids.

Jacobi said that a climber can never be confident of whether they are risking the "fall of three metres," which Paul said was of lesser sporting value, or risking the rope-snapping plummet to the death that Paul said had a higher sporting value, regardless of the number of pitons.

Paul responded in January 1912, in the issue of the *German Alpine Times* following the one in which he responded to Nieberl. "An evaluation of the few arguments that Jacobi has presented not based on mistaken interpretations is something I can largely spare myself," Paul wrote.[170] "[Jacobi is] characteristic of the weak, decadent type of modern mountaineer who goes to the mountains so as to numb his shattered nerves by means of intense impressions. Physically and mentally sound, strong men belong on mountain routes! But if, during the overcoming of a hard climb, anyone really thinks of the difficulties that the body-recovery expedition will encounter, then a person should, if he is not so prudent as to give up climbing on his own, be forbidden the mountains and be placed in a sanitarium for nervous conditions."[171]

Paul inverted Jacobi's insinuation that he sought to strip climbers of the past of their achievements. "Following my principles seems to me to require falling back from an attained but illusionary height of relative performance, and many a person would, regarding routes he had carried out according to his old method, today feel something like a pang of conscience. Certainly, giving up an acquired height is difficult; this we mountain climbers know for certain, and the millionaire accepts more modest circumstances with difficulty too. I also don't want to cross the paths of the 'veterans' and compel them to deeds which they either ought not to expect of themselves or which would humble them."[172]

He attached his six theses and concluded with a romantic plea for climbers to halt modern technology at the gates of alpinism. "If alpinism has a future in which it is to hold its own even against cable railways and trips by airship, then it lies in the *alpine* sport [and not in pitons and other aids] we uphold because we love it."[173]

In an editor's note after Paul's response, Schmidkunz wrote that there would be no more articles on the subject in his paper. "The Munich Bayerland chapter of the Alpine Club will hold a public discussion meeting on this topic at the end of January, which we will report on in due course."[174]

Schmidkunz sponsored the debate and set the date for January 31. Hans Dülfer, who reported on the event for the Alpine Club,[175] noted that the city's climbers had been preoccupied with the pending debate, and the mood in the meeting room of the Bayerland Section was intense.[176] Indeed, among the audience and guest speakers were some of the most opinionated and experienced rock climbers in Europe, all ready to passionately dispute the future of climbing.

Franz Nieberl and Paul Jacobi formed the core of the opposition. Tita, who by now had worked himself into a state in which he described the rejection of pitons as a "barbarous absurdity," had been invited. On January 12, however, his wife had died of peritonitis. After her death, the Leipzig Section tried to evict Tita and his daughters, Olga, Pia and Carmela, from the Vajolet hut, the only home they had known, and he could not afford to leave the premises for long. Tita's absence from the debate was also unfortunate because he understood Paul better than anyone, and Paul looked up to him.

Eugen Oertel,[177] a lawyer and mountaineering writer as well as the chair of the Bayerland Section, introduced Paul, who spoke briefly on his theses, then gave the lectern to Nieberl.

To the surprise of Dülfer and, doubtless, Paul, Nieberl had changed his tone and his views. Instead of personal attacks, he agreed with Paul, although with regret, that rock climbing had "emancipated" itself from alpinism, as was evident not just on the Elbsandsteingebirge in Saxony, but in the limestone Alps as well. Nieberl now believed that climbers should be superior and not just equal to the route they chose. He also agreed that climbers should only climb up where they can downclimb, although he emphasized (as did Paul) that safe downclimbing required memorizing the climb carefully on the way up. Nieberl also agreed with Paul that artificial aids should be reserved for emergencies. He thought it self-evident that pitons were not to comprise the main basis for an ascent. Finally, he said that limiting abseiling and the use of the rope for tension traverses and other manoeuvres might be correct in principle, but the application was to be left to the climber's discretion.

The problem, as Nieberl now saw it, was the definition of an emergency that justified the use of aids. Must it be a death or serious injury, or would lesser crises like being caught in a storm, or the onset of nightfall and an unplanned open bivouac, qualify? Nieberl agreed that security was the highest principle of climbing, although he was worried by Paul's qualification that this did not include "the frantic correction of one's own insecurity." After all, this had always been the principle behind the use of aids, and Paul made no allowance for the use of protection to guard against "unforeseen happenstance."[178]

Nieberl ended by saying that in the mountains "everyone should follow their own path to happiness," which could be taken as both a conciliatory gesture and an apology for his earlier remarks.[179] Paul must have wondered what kind of man had called him perverse, a Moloch, a bacillus, a spreader of false doctrines and a destroyer of youth when he seemed to agree with him on the matters that had inspired these insults.

Jacobi, the next speaker, was more aggressive. "You want this as a rule: no rope and no pitons," said Jacobi, "but aren't frank enough to declare this openly, partly because you yourself feel that it's absurd and immoral and partly because you yourself, at least when you climb with others, aren't able to dispense with this useful thing."[180] Once again, Jacobi missed the mark. Although Paul did not openly discuss his piton use in the debate, he had not tried to hide it. He had admitted to using pitons on the Trisselwand in November in the *Styrian Alpine Post*.

Paul Hübel, an author, publisher and proponent of unguided climbing, endorsed Paul's theses – with the caveat that aids be used in the face of anticipated as well as present danger, such as the onset of a storm. He saw a "danger" in the "radical separation" of rock climbing from alpinism, however, presumably because he thought that if rock climbing lost the moral compass of mountaineering traditions, aids such as pitons would proliferate.[181]

By the time Georg Leuchs, who had climbed the mighty South Face of the Marmolada, took his turn, Dülfer said there was "general tension" in the room. Leuchs agreed with Preuss, but he also advised the use of protection "where advisable," not just in emergencies. He conceded with Preuss and Nieberl that rock climbing was an independent sport but thought that a better definition of fair practice was needed. In a rare lighter moment on that serious evening, he commented that "the difference between Piaz, Nieberl and Preuss seems to lie only in the fact that Piaz will permit perhaps thirty, Nieberl perhaps three, but Preuss no pitons at all."[182]

In his closing remarks, Paul reassured the crowd that as "harmonious as possible unification" of rock and alpine climbing was desirable. Downclimbing, he said, should only be tried after much practice. To fulfill the ideal of good climbing, guidelines must be codified into clearly understood "moral rules" for those who are unable to make their own good decisions about how to climb. "The distinction between artificial and natural aids, between fair and unfair lies to be sure, as stressed by almost every speaker, in the mountaineer's sense of tact, but it is also this feeling that clearly differentiates as to whether one is, as leader, also using the link formed by the rope in order to get up the mountain or precisely because one is climbing the mountain."[183]

With that statement, Paul drew an enduring line between aid and free climbing. It was a philosophical breakthrough in climbing equal to Purtscheller's separation of objective and subjective dangers. The theses founded a moral code by which Winkler's romantic, self-abnegating act of scaling the mountain became a moral, philosophical and sporting pursuit. The earliest alpinists had followed the path Paul proposed because they had few other options, but Paul put the experience of free climbing at the heart of climbing.

The Marquess of Queensberry Rules mitigated the possible harm to boxers by guaranteeing civility in a brutal sport. Paul's six theses sought to maintain the risk of harm in a sport threatened not by brutality but civilization. His theses put the climber's vulnerability to failure and even injury or death at the existential core of climbing.

Paul began the 1912 season as the victor in a battle that had put his reputation as a climber and a man on the line. The process by which he had achieved his status as a climber and then defended it had been as demanding as many doctoral dissertations. Perhaps not coincidentally, around this time he began to use the title of doctor.

The seasons ahead would take him from the limestone Alps to the high peaks of the Mont Blanc range. The most dramatic and useful immediate personal outcome for Paul, however, was that he had discovered a talent and a passion for writing and presenting on mountain subjects. His graduate studies were faltering, and he was beginning to consider other fields of study, when the controversy allowed him to discover a whole new career. On a personal level, however, the victory in the controversy may have been pyrrhic for Paul. Now he climbed in the public eye as the prophet of his own merciless ideals.

Doctor Preuss Presents

*Dr. Paul Preuss, in order to prevent any inquiries
[for free presentations], regrets that he is only
able to make presentations on alpine or skiing
subjects in exchange for remuneration.*

—handbill, 1912

Between 1912 and 1913, Paul made more than 150 presentations to Alpine Club sections, ski clubs, unaffiliated groups
of climbers, skiers and nature lovers. The venues ranged
from huts to concert halls, but most of his talks were in humble
rented beer cellars or halls far from the mountains, where he was
the main attraction at monthly meetings. The audience was predominantly tired men who came directly to the bar in their crum-
pled suits from 12-hour shifts in offices. Unless the section was in
a mountain town like Kufstein, Innsbruck or Munich, most of its
members visited the Alps once a year on their summer vacation.[184]
Such audiences were charmed to find that despite their daily, city-
bound, lowland lives, they were fellow travellers with this formally
dressed, thin-haired speaker with a slight overbite and a fearsome
climbing record.

The audience nodded gravely when Paul spoke of matters like
handholds, the chance of snow in a certain range at a certain time
of year, or some minor misadventure, but the mood was not always serious. Paul showed lantern slides of snowfields, rock peaks
and climbers in action, accompanying these not only with descrip-
tive explanations but also with jokes and unscripted commentary
on everything from the difficulties of rock climbing to the humble
realities of hut life. Paul often made light of himself and encouraged the audience to do the same. Many audience members later
recalled that he was the best presenter they had seen.

Paul inadvertently discovered an extensive, underserviced market for entertainment at evening club meetings. Evening meetings

were an important part of the life of clubs and sections that were often in considerable debt or needed members to help pay for the repair and upkeep of huts and trails – so much so that some sections made attendance a requirement of membership. Without an occasional reminder of the glories of alpinism, mountain fervour in urban members lapsed, along with their membership and dues.

But how to provide these entertainments? A few sections had climbing or skiing skills requirements for membership, but many more had conditions based on politics, religion, level of education or social status. The largest sections were based in cities and had few members immersed in the latest climbing developments of interest.

Wealthier sections held costume balls. Members came dressed as *Senners*, woodsmen, mountain guides or village priests, and the men were forbidden to wear costume gloves or to arrive in their "bicycling attire." Women were exhorted "to leave their diamonds at home" and to wear the dirndl.[185] Papier-mâché rocks and tableaux of crags and pine trees decorated meeting halls to complete the effect. Attendees enjoyed patriotic songs, folk music and sometimes fireworks.

These evenings celebrated the Alps as a charming, exotic place where culture and history had come to a halt – a seductive, anti-modernist trope for the well-to-do. The climbers who threw themselves at the local *Klettergarten* walls and aspired to the latest *Klettersport* routes, however, were mostly tradesmen and mid-level office employees. They formed or joined sections preoccupied with serious technical climbing, and their evening meetings reflected their view of the Alps as a place of change.

Italian climber Aldo Bonacossa, a student in Munich in the 1900s, attended the evening meetings of serious climbing clubs, including the Bayerland Section, to which Hans Dülfer and Paul also belonged. He was amused to see the presenters, whom he compared to tragic Wagnerian heroes, spinning yarns about storm-slashed alpine struggles in cozy beer cellars full of warm, dry and pleasantly drunk city-based mountaineers.[186]

Sections focused on modern technical climbing or skiing had an even harder time acquiring speakers than sections mostly devoted to hiking and scrambling. Organizers who read the *German Alpine Times* were pleased to learn that the dashing young climber, who had taken a stand for climbing style and soloed what few could climb even with a rope, was willing to offer presentations on subjects both current and traditional.

Bonacossa said that "the cheerful Viennese" pleasantly surprised audiences steeled for another night of tales of alpine storm and sorrow.[187] Günther von Saar attributed Paul's popularity as a lecturer to his ability to read the mood and interests of audiences.

As Paul's certainty about becoming a biology professor declined, he expanded his syllabus of potential lectures to encompass subjects as diverse as winter sports, skiing, climbing technique and hunting. Each lecture had an intriguing title, such as "Alpinism and Non-Alpinism," "Alpinism in Our Country and Other Countries," "Danger and Difficulty in Alpinism," "Old-style Winter Tours," "My Most Beautiful Mountain Tours," "Winter on Germany's Highest Peak," and "The Handling of the Rope."[188] In addition to the usual mountain art and stock photos of the alpine landscape, Paul showed slides made from his own snapshots, a modern novelty.

Serious photography involved heavy cameras, tripods and delicate 30-by-40-centimetre glass slides, all of which required skill, care and training to use in ordinary settings. Most photographers who lugged all of this equipment up to a ledge or a glacier to shoot mountains or climbers could not afford to gamble on whether a worthwhile action shot presented itself. Professional mountain photographers like the Italian Vittorio Sella overcame these technical challenges to create some of the most stunning photographs of mountains ever taken. Action photographs of climbers, however, were so rare that even earnest alpinists like Georg Winkler were forced to pose for portraits in studios decorated with alpine props.

Georges Tairraz from Chamonix, Fritz Gratl from Innsbruck, Alwin Keil from Dresden and a few other photographers posed climbers on rocks or mountains in the style of the tableaux popular in studios and shot them frozen in place. Slow shutter speeds made these shoots so rare and difficult that publishers and presenters usually relied on illustrators such as Gustav Jahn and Otto Barth to capture the experience of climbers in action.

Paul joined a revolution in photography that eventually swept away the fake rocks and painted backdrops. In 1900, Kodak had introduced the small, inexpensive, hand-held Brownie camera. The Brownie Number 2 had a light, strong aluminum body, was easy to handle and loaded cheap roll film. Six-shot rolls and a home development kit cost a pittance. What hand-held cameras lacked in image quality they made up for by allowing amateur photographers to capture spontaneous action.

Austrian *Bergfreund* Joseph August Lux's essay "Artistic Secrets of the Kodak" enjoined Kodak users to avoid studio-style photographs that reproduced natural settings and compositions and aped paintings. "We do not want to show nature in its customary format," Lux said, "but we want to surprise it at one of its interesting unpredictabilities, one that is novel to us and original and offers an unexpected aspect of the otherwise so blatant commonplace of persons and objects."[189]

Paul's slides were so unique that he mentioned them in his advertisement for his lectures. They included pictures of himself taken by his climbing partners, and his own shots of climbing, landscapes, friends and his family, often in traditional dress. He also took several pictures of abseiling and ropework that hinted at a fascination with the slings, ropes and techniques he had so strongly condemned.

The most famous photos of Paul were taken in the Dolomites, the Kaisergebirge and the Gesäuse in 1911. A few of them looked composed, along the lines of Gustav Jahn's illustrations. In one such photo, Paul stood on a ledge, looking outwards to a valley; in another, he leaned casually against a summit cairn. In these, as in all but a couple of other images, Paul wore a suit.

There were also snapshots that made up for their lack of composition or even lens focus with their immediacy. In a photo taken on the vertical rock of the Sassolungo, the rope hung free from Paul's waist as he led. There was no protection, and the rock above looked difficult. A shot of Paul slinking up the overhanging crack of the Schiefer Riss on the Totenkirchl showed his crack technique, and his footwork looked perfect on a slab on the North Face of the Hochtor, given the evident lack of good handholds. Then there was the photo of Paul looking up at the Campanile Basso's East Face before he soloed it.

The winter lecture schedule of 1913 was even busier than that of 1912. Paul's calendar for January and February alone was packed. On January 10, he gave a lecture in Munich on the subject of expert climbers. On the evenings of January 23 to 25, he spoke to the socialist Bergfrei Section on ski touring in the Silvretta range and climbing on the Tre Cime di Lavaredo. On January 30, he lectured to the Munich Academic Section on rock and ice climbing. The next day, he spoke to the Bayerland Section on artificial aids. On February 2 and 3, he spoke to the University of Munich during their ski trip to Garmisch-Partenkirchen. On February 13, he lectured on the Langkofel group to the Alpen Section. On February 14, he spoke to the Munich Touring Club about climbing in the Wilder Kaiser, and on February 15 to the Munich Section on the subject of the Dachstein. On February 16, he delivered a presentation on the Grossglockner to the Klub Alpiner Skiläufer.

By the end of 1912, the presentation business was a major source of Paul's income. He had even printed out a handbill advertising his services and the terms he required:

> Dr. Paul Preuss, in order to prevent any inquiries [for free presentations], regrets that he is only able to make presentations on alpine or skiing subjects in exchange for remuneration. The fee for the lecture is 100 marks (or, in Austria, 100 kronen) plus travel and lodging expenses in the amount of 15 marks (or kronen) per 100 kilometres of railway travel (from Munich). For all of the lectures, light images, for the most part [his own] will be used. Wishes of the clubs with regard to the content of the lectures are considered as far as possible. Communications requested Dr. P. Preuss, Altaussee, Styria, Austria. For January 1914, a lecture tour through Northern Germany is planned.

Paul's fee of 100 marks translated to about $800 in today's US dollars; a junior university professor in 1910 made about 450 marks a year, the modern equivalent of $36,000. Günther von Saar claimed that in the three-year period between 1911 and fall 1913, Preuss lectured 100 times, which would have earned him at least 10,000 marks, or about six times the annual salary of an untenured lecturer.

Paul now made his living writing articles and giving lectures. Over a two-year period, he authored some 32 articles published in Schmidkunz's papers as well as the organs of club sections, the Alpine Club itself and local publications like the *Styrian Alpine Post*. Although his career as a mountain writer had begun with the fiery first article in the Piton Controversy, his reputation as a presenter was more bourgeois. A photograph of Paul in his study in his flat at 92 Adalbertstrasse portrayed him as a climber and a man of letters. He sat cross-legged in front of a writing desk and mused at an ice axe he held in one hand, while he tucked the other in his waistcoat pocket. It is the image of the romantic writer recalling the intense emotion of a climb or a beautiful vista, not in rags and a garret, but in the safety of a fine suit of clothes and a comfortable study, as befitted the most popular German-language climbing writer of his day.

Despite this staid image, Paul continued to find controversies irresistible and took sides on problems as diverse as the use of huts in the winter, professionalism in skiing, and relations between backcountry users and hunters. Yet he never lost sight of his core audience of rock climbers and wrote about technical difficulties with increasing skill.

"A bulge projecting from the wall must be surmounted at its low-point and to reach it, a delicate traverse must be made under overhangs,"[190] was just one such sentence in several pages of description of technical rock climbing manoeuvres in his article "The North Ridge of the Grossen Ödsteins," typical of his numerous articles on climbs and trip reports. *Klettersport* fanatics would have had sweaty palms when they read his description of his first ascent of the East Face of the Campanile Basso: "Through an overhanging yellow section, and right onto a wall... incredibly steep. Then up a narrow band of rock to overhangs and bearing right to a yellow niche, where

I left a cairn and a note... very exposed, very difficult wall climbing."[191]

Paul also explored the psychological and ethical dimensions of climbing, with unusual skill. In a report on the first ascent of the North Wall of the Gross Litzner, he described the mental process of soloing, during which he struggled with "the most hidden games of his thoughts."[192] At times, the psychological tension was high. He wrote about how, as he and Relly put on their crampons below the North Face of the Trafoier Eiswand's Bäckmann Ridge, they both realized that their timing was poor, but that they would attempt the climb anyway.[193] Earlier writers like Winkler and Lammer did not question their impulse to experience self-immolation in nature, but Paul always acknowledged the complex relationship between self-doubt and commitment.

He was also, however, resistant to hyperbole and an expert satirist. "Despite many attempts," he wrote, in his account of the first ascent of North Ridge of the Grossen Ödsteins, "I have never learned the technique of climbing a 'blank wall devoid of hand and footholds' about which one reads so frequently, so there were hand and footholds here."[194]

Growing up in Altaussee gave Paul a better understanding of alpine village life than his urban audiences had. Most mountaineers lived in rapidly growing cities with increasing problems of overcrowding and pollution. They saw the mountains as either a rocky playground or a pristine, unspoiled reserve of nature where society was homogeneous and governed by quaint customs.[195] Paul, however, personally knew the different points of view of the loggers, miners and Senners who were mostly invisible to weekend hut guests. In "The Kaiser Monument," he described how the inhabitants of an alpine town were at cross-purposes when they decided to erect a bust of the emperor. The different groups all had their own ideas about where it should be placed and where the kaiser should appear to gaze. A last-minute donation from the baron settled the latter issue: the kaiser would look towards the manor house. Nature, however, could eventually overrule the will of both villagers and kaiser "if the wind turns the Emperor around."[196]

Although village life appeared on occasion in Paul's work, he preferred to write about the natural beauty of the mountains beyond the meadows and farms. Emotions inspired by wildflowers, animals and sunsets abounded in his writing. Paul had moved from the amateur botany of his father to an affective spirituality of nature shared by the likes of Pastor Selle. His nature writing expanded his appeal to casual *Bergfreunde* and nature lovers. "We stopped a speedy descent," Paul said, "to look on in silent joy and wonder at slender chamois" who were "shy" and "wide-eyed."[197] Spring crocuses "created a splendid, colourful festive scene."[198] Snowfields "bathed in a sea of light" and made "rows of hollow troughs, hill upon hill covered by glittering masses of snow."[199]

These articles built Paul's reputation as a climber and a man of letters sensitive to the varied groups of mountain enthusiasts, and thus gained him his broadest possible audience. He had become one of the first professional climbers, and in the lore- and legend-driven world of alpinism, his reputation was secure. Yet Paul was in his mid-20s and at the height of his climbing powers, with a drive fuelled by a relentless need to prove himself.

Life as a Trifle: The Kaisergebirge, Northern Limestone and the Western Alps, 1912-13

Others will climb it, I renounce it.

—Paul Preuss, on the South Ridge of
the Aiguille Noire de Peuterey

The genuine madman [Paul Preuss] to whom I was roped up, gave up and I took the lead, which at least meant I could climb as sanely as I pleased. After all, I had promised his mother I would bring him back alive, and I always at least try to keep my word, even when it comes to trifles.

—Tita Piaz

A busy lecture season did not keep Paul out of the mountains. In a five-week period in February and March of 1912, Paul gave 11 presentations and also made ski ascents of nine mountains and completed several one- and two-day ski tours. He even made a long ski tour in early January in the Kaisergebirge and arranged for Emmy Eisenberg, Mina, and Paul Relly to join him.

Paul's lecture circuit offered new contacts and climbing opportunities. In 1912, he met 22-year-old Count Ugo di Vallepiana, an Italian studying economics in Munich. Both men had Jewish, mountain-loving fathers, but whereas Paul's family were bourgeois, Vallepiana's had been ennobled by King Umberto I in 1880 for their banking services to the crown.

Vallepiana preferred the mountains to the neoclassical splendour of the Ottolenghi di Vallepiana palace, where he had spent his childhood. He had been a mountaineering prodigy, albeit a much better funded one than Paul, who had lacked money even for hut fees as a boy. Excellent guides accompanied the teenage

Vallepiana on the Matterhorn and an early ascent of 3650-metre Point Budden in the Murailles. He also shared Paul's love of solo climbing, and at 21 he soloed the Brouillard Ridge on Mont Blanc. Vallepiana and Paul were a natural team, and they made plans to meet again in the summer in Courmayeur.

In mid-June, Paul took up residence at Strips in the Kaisergebirge to train on difficult rock climbs for a big season in the Mont Blanc range. He brought an entourage, including Emmy Eisenberg; Walter Schmidkunz; Grete Loew, for whose sake he had used pitons on the Trisselwand; Walter Bing; and the talented Rudi Redlich, with whom had climbed a new route on the Torre Est in the Catinaccio group the year before. Paul and his friends found Hans Dülfer already at Strips with Hanne Franz and Werner Schaarschmidt.

Dülfer had seen Paul at the Piton Controversy debate and knew all about his climbs and philosophies. Dülfer had just completed the first ascent of the East Face of the Fleischbank. Although Dülfer had inspected routes on abseil and used rope tension and pitons on many of his climbs, Paul befriended him and introduced him to his circle.[200]

On June 28, Paul and Dülfer, accompanied by Schmidkunz, Eisenberg and Franz, climbed the difficult North Ridge of the Predigtstuhl. It was the only time the two experts climbed together. Schmidkunz, the first but not the last climbing magazine editor to create a rivalry out of nothing, photographed them on the same, long, out-of-balance move on the vertical ridge and published the photos together. Dülfer looks a hair's breadth closer to perfect balance and control than Paul. There was no jealousy or rivalry between them, however. Dülfer's specialization was hard rock, and Paul saw himself first and foremost as an alpinist, a separate discipline of which rock climbing was but one component.

A few days later, a slip on a talus descent gave Paul a painful hematoma on one of his ankles. A doctor in Kufstein warned him to avoid straining his ankles for the rest of the season. Paul's spontaneous healing from polio, however, had made him a lifelong skeptic of modern medicine. Instead of resting, he soloed a difficult route on the Kleine Halt and made a speed ascent of the Heroldweg on the Totenkirchl before he returned to Altaussee.

After visiting with Lina and answering correspondence about lectures and articles, Paul set out for Courmayeur for his first season in the Mont Blanc range, the highest mountains of Europe. Biographer Severino Casara unleashed his imagination to describe the farewell. "The embrace of his sad mother is more painful than the last glimpse of his native mountains. Bent under his enormous pack, before he disappears among the trees, he turns and says, '*Arrivederci*, Mama! *Arrivederci* at the end of August!' Sophie and Mina run to the gate and follow him as far as the bridge over the river Traun."[201]

Paul was going to Mont Blanc both for his love of climbing and to make a name for himself. Climbers from the limestone ranges had completed the hardest rock climbs in the Alps, but in a global context their efforts had a slightly avant-garde and suspect quality next to the world-famous climbs on the granite aiguilles and massive snow and ice faces of the Mont Blanc range. A climber who had made their name in this range had no need to further prove themselves in the limestone Alps, but the same could not be said of a climber whose ascents had been limited to the mountains of Austria, Italy or Germany.

The golden age of alpinism was marked by the conquest of the most famous peaks in the Alps and ended with the first ascent of the Matterhorn in 1865. The silver age followed, with ascents of more difficult, lower, less well-known locally named peaks, and ended with the controversial ascent of the Dent du Géant. Some of the most spectacular climbs of the silver age had been completed in the Mont Blanc range, including the Petit Dru, the Grands Charmoz, the Droites and the Aiguille Noire de Peuterey.

A creative, final age of alpinism had dawned in the Mont Blanc range. Peaks, faces, aiguilles and ridges that distinguished themselves only in the eyes of alpinists would be explored and named by a new kind of climber armed with skills and techniques unknown just a few decades before. It was an approach that favoured climbers like Paul, with his honed skills, drive, *Schneid* and familiarity with climbing on untravelled terrain.

Chamonix later became more famous as the home base of alpinism in the Mont Blanc range, but in 1912, Courmayeur was equally popular with mountaineers. It was also an obvious first choice for Paul. He spoke Italian, several of his friends made annual pilgrimages there, and sections of the Alpine Club to which he belonged organized vacations there during the climbing season. Despite Courmayeur's popularity, it was Paul's first trip to Italy, and in a flush of enthusiasm, he joined the Italian Alpine Club.

He arrived on July 22. It had been raining for days in Courmayeur. Climbers moped around campsites, hotels, bars and boulders, waiting for the snow, which came down to 2500 metres, to melt. Paul made the best of it. He'd had little contact with the climbing world beyond the Alps to the east, and the bad weather gave him an opportunity to meet alpinists from around the world. Among them was top British climber Geoffrey Winthrop Young. In a move a certain type of Viennese climber would have considered a faux pas, he brought his expert Swiss guide, Josef Knubel. Young was quite capable of unguided climbing, but like many British climbers, he enjoyed having a member of what he called a "peasant aristocracy... a status familiar to Englishmen, that of the huntsman or gamekeeper, with a dash of tiger-hunter thrown in," tied to his rope.[202]

Although a few British clients complained that their guides lacked skill and commitment, the results of many client-guide teams tell another story. Young's 1906 first ascent of the South Face of the Täschhorn with Irish climber Valentine (V.J.E.) Ryan and guides Franz, Gabriel and Joseph Lochmatter was only repeated in 1942, with pitons and more advanced ice gear. The guides played a key role in leading the cruxes. Young and Josef Knubel made the first ascent of the West Ridge of Grandes Jorasses. One of Young and Knubel's hardest climbs was the Mer de Glace face of the Grépon in 1911, on which they were joined by Courmayeur guide Alexis Brocherel, ace English rock climber and actuary Ralph Todhunter and Humphrey Owen (H.O.) Jones, one of the best rock climbers in Wales. The Grépon itself was first climbed in 1881 by Englishman Albert Mummery, guided by Alexander Burgener and Benedikt Venetz. Knubel's eponymous crack was the hardest pitch in the Mont Blanc range at the time, as difficult as the crux on the West Face of the Totenkirchl or any pitch in the Eastern Alps.

Jones had already made his reputation in the Mont Blanc range with gruelling ascents of long ridges such as the traverse of the Triolets, which comprised numerous high peaks and technical traverses. Jones completed his longest projects by climbing the individual components separately over several seasons before eventually ascending the whole project in one push. In 1912, he had returned to Courmayeur for more, along with his partners on the Triolets, Karl Blodig and the Anglo-German engineer and eccentric Oscar Eckenstein.

Eckenstein's Jewish heritage, technical views about climbing technique and left-wing politics had put him on the fringes of the Alpine Club in London. He was also suspected of not being a proper chap because he had joined occultist and alpinist Aleister Crowley on his 1902 attempt on K2. But he was fascinated by the technological and scientific problems of climbing. Young credited Eckenstein with teaching him how to improve his balance by bouldering. He was also knowledgeable about machining and metallurgy. He invented the strong, stable, two-piece modern crampon suited to climbing ice without cutting steps, and he shortened the ice axe from about a metre and a half to 80 centimetres so that it could be used with one hand on steep ice.[203] Before these innovations, snow slopes were climbed by chopping hundreds of steps. City-raised climbers found this so onerous and laborious that they had guides do it for them. Now, with a little practice and good snow, a climber could ascend quickly by gripping the slope with crampon points and using the pick of the axe for additional traction. In the right conditions, the savings in strength allowed skilled climbers to move quickly and avoid falling rock. Eckenstein's crampons soon became standard for serious ice climbers.

The British were divided over the issue of guides, but most shared Paul's belief that the rope tricks and pitons banned from the British Isles had no place in the Alps either. British climbing's philosophies came closer to Paul's ethics than those of continental alpinism. Young's 600-page treatise *Mountain Craft* confidently stated on behalf of the climbers of Britain that "artificial aids have never been popular with us. If a climber does not feel safe in descending, he ought to practice on rock he can climb, not spoil rock he cannot, with blacksmith's leavings [pitons].... Pegs to hammer in and anchor to are a remedy for our failures... Their use is corrective then, not auxiliary..."[204] A piton "is no protection for a leader, although its insertion may tempt him to perilously go beyond what he should."[205] Young's comparison of climbing with pitons to gymnastics closely parallels Paul's own words on the subject.

Although Paul was an acknowledged master in the Eastern Alps, the top British climbers and their guides were more accomplished on the mixed ice, snow and rock of the Mont Blanc range. Paul was a fast learner, however, and Jones and Young confirmed his biases and exposed him to new ideas. That summer, Paul began an enchainment project that would have impressed Jones. He adopted Eckenstein's ice gear and, despite his devotion to guideless climbing's philosophers, began to admire guides.

The poor weather continued, and the sky never cleared long enough for big climbs to come into condition. Paul climbed moderate routes on the Aiguille du Châtelet, Mont Chétif, Mont Brise and Tête de Bernarde, but these were not the grand objectives that had brought him to Courmayeur.

On August 12, Paul tired of waiting in town and hiked up to the Gamba hut (since replaced by the Monzino hut) to wait for the next break in the weather. From there, if the weather broke, he could choose from dozens of spectacular climbs, including the unclimbed South Ridge of the Aiguille Noire de Peuterey, the pillars of the Dames Anglaises, the 4108-metre-high Aiguille Blanche de Peuterey, the Aiguille Croux and the Innominata and Brouillard ridges.

The tiny hut was already crowded. H.O. Jones was there with his wife of two weeks, Muriel Gwendolen Edwards, and their experienced guide, Julius Truffer. The day before, they had pulled off the first ascent of the north summit of the Dames Anglaises. The crack team of Young and Knubel, however, had been waiting at the Gamba for days, hoping in vain for an improvement in conditions.

Young and Paul were both idealists and writers with much to discuss. They would soon climb together, and Young's later writings showed that he understood Paul's ideas about climbing style and his penchant for soloing. On August 13, however, the weather remained poor, and Young and Knubel gave up and left for Courmayeur. Paul stayed on with the Joneses' party and hoped for the best.

August 15 dawned clear but cold, with snow down to 3000 metres, rendering higher objectives out of condition. Paul and the Joneses' party teamed up for the only route free of snow: Mont Rouge de Peuterey, a rocky peak at the foot of the Peuterey Ridge that stood less than 3000 metres high. Paul would not have bothered with it in good conditions. Paul would solo in front, unroped, to find the best route, and the others would follow on a rope led by Truffer.

The climbing began in earnest at a shoulder between Mont Rouge itself and the unclimbed South Ridge of the Aiguille Noire. Gwendolen roped up between Truffer, who would lead the climb, and her husband, who would follow and offer encouragement.[206] During the Piton Controversy, Paul had discussed how a less skilled climber endangered a whole roped party. Now he proposed that Gwendolen should come last, to double the chances of Jones and Truffer catching a fall that could pull all three climbers off the mountain. It was not Paul's decision to make, however, and Jones insisted that Gwendolen remain in the middle of the rope.

The climbing was moderate, and Paul compared the difficulties to the well-trodden *Führerweg* on the Totenkirchl. Halfway to the summit, Truffer told his rope mates to wait as he exited a chimney. Six metres above, Paul paused and watched Truffer. Gwendolen stood on a ledge two metres below Truffer and waited for the guide's signal to commence climbing. Fifteen metres of slack rope separated her from her husband, who stood a few metres below her.

Truffer's handholds suddenly broke. He fell and instantly

plucked the others off the mountain; they fell 300 metres to the Fresnay glacier and their deaths.

Many artists had depicted the demise of whole roped parties. The famous Matterhorn fatality in which Douglas Hadow fell and pulled Francis Douglas, Charles Hudson and Michel Croz with him, was perhaps the most popular subject in mountaineering art. In typical renditions, the climbers braced themselves, dangled for a moment as the rope tugged at their waist, or expressed momentary horror before succumbing to their inescapable fate.[207] Paul saw none of that. "There was no holding on while dangling from the rope," he said, "and other romantic nonsense that has subsequently been reported. The next day, with difficulty, three heavily mutilated corpses were recovered."[208]

Paul guessed that Truffer had assumed the granite holds were stable. On the loose limestone of the Eastern Alps, climbers tended to equalize their weight and avoid committing to a single hold, a technique that Paul saw as more important than belaying.[209] Paul also thought that, unlike the Eastern Alps, where the routes were shorter but more consistently steep, Mont Blanc presented "five difficult metres in a hundred," so climbers tended not to slow down and climb with caution on the short, hard sections.

During the Piton Controversy, Paul had said that parties would be better off unroped if there were any risk that the entire team could be lost in the case of a fall. The accident vindicated his opinion, but Paul's suggestion beforehand had been merely that the weakest climber come last, which would have given Jones at least a chance to catch Truffer's fall. Paul also reported that the party had been so close together that there was no way to brace for the impact of the fall or secure the rope over a bollard, if one had been available.

After the accident, Paul was more empathetic towards other climbers. A year before, he had dismissed a grim, colourful warning from Tita about what it felt like when a climbing partner died in the mountains. In his report on this, his first encounter with death in the mountains, Paul expressed a new emotional depth. The mountains he loved so much could not be made totally secure by clever climbing. The "mutilated corpses," of which he later learned from Young, who led the recovery party, proved that Tita had been right. What Paul loved more than anything else in the world could hurt and kill after all. Paul had mocked Jacobi for writing that every climber fears death, even on the safest fall. Now he counselled guides to improve their professional standards and scheduled a charity lecture in Courmayeur on behalf of their insurance fund. Empathy welled up in Paul from an origin deeper than recent trauma. Pain gave eloquence to a childhood dread of the darkness of mountains. Because the peaks could kill, they could also inspire the compassion that ennobled climbing and life itself.

On August, 21, Paul crossed the Colle del Gigante and spent three days waiting out the weather on the French side of Mont Blanc, where he reunited with Young. Paul and the Englishman now shared a talent for climbing, an approach to its philosophies and involvement in a tragedy. When they parted at the Couvercle hut, they doubtless anticipated climbing together in the future.

Paul made his last climb in the Mont Blanc range in 1912: the Aiguille de l'Évêque, by himself. It was yet another minor peak, less than 4000 metres high, chosen by default because of bad weather.

On August 23, Paul wrote from Courmayeur to Aldo Bonacossa in Milan. He complained that his clothes were in disorder and that few climbs were in condition. In a rare post-university admission of interest in another sport, he claimed that "at the end of June [1913], I will race in the Kehres car in the Tyrolean Austrian Alpine Race."[210] Long-distance alpine car races like the 2900-kilometre Tyrolean trial of 1913 were popular with motoring fans. But Paul's interest was short-lived; he never competed.

On August 27, Paul returned to Altaussee to recover from his difficult season and spend time with his family. He busied himself with paperwork and planned his winter lecture itinerary until good fall conditions in the Styrian Alps tempted him away from his desk. The ensuing frenzy of climbing included 11 enchainments and other ascents adding up to more than 40 summits, including ten in a single effort with Viennese climber Karl Richter.

Paul had grown up in the shadow of the West Face of the Trisselwand, the "gloomy" mountain wall of his childhood, the birthplace of local technical rock climbing and the mountain where he had compromised his principles. The face was one of Paul's favourite climbs. That autumn alone, he climbed it with his old friend Relly and his sister Mina, now Relly's wife; twice in one day with Karl Richter; once via the more difficult Reinl Route; and once in snowy conditions with local friend Christl Kerry. Paul even used the climb to show off to local sisters Elly and Karin Benedickt, whom he took up the route separately on the same day.

Paul began his 1912 lecture season on November 10 in Munich. Two days later, he lectured in Strasbourg, the hometown of Lina and his college friend Walter Bing. With Bing, he climbed the stairs of the 300-metre cathedral tower, visited the rocks of the Spitzekoepfe and spent the night in a tent on the Hohneck. Stern mountaineers like Zsigmondy looked back on their early rural (rather than alpine) hiking excursions with a mixture of embarrassment and bemusement. Paul, now a famous climber with his own income, still had a charming, boyish enthusiasm for humble outdoor adventures.

Paul's lecture itinerary took him all over Germany and Austria, and at the end of December, he returned to Altaussee for the holidays. He spent Christmas with his family and invited his sisters and several friends, including Paul Relly and Emmy Eisenberg, to stay over on New Year's Eve for a celebratory bonfire and skiing. Forty-five years later, Eisenberg told Casara:

> They stacked the wood for the bonfire, singing in the evening, but [Paul] appeared to be in a bad mood. He was distant and indifferent. His eyes were fixed on the sky, where the full moon hung above a fir tree and the mountains beyond. He exclaimed, by way of an apology [for his mood], "Ah, Emmy!"
>
> In the solitude of the winter night, the mountains and the meadows looked small compared to the fir tree. In that mute conversation with the stars, did the silent thunder of his soul remind him that the spirit was reserved for much higher summits than those of earth? He followed me slowly back to the others. When the bonfire

died down, we went into the hut, and as we slept, January 1, 1913, dawned.[211]

Eisenberg and some of Paul's friends retroactively interpreted some of his words or moods as fatalistic, but there is a simpler explanation. Paul had much to look forward to in 1913, including a busy lecture schedule in January and February, ambitious ski mountaineering objectives in the Western Alps and a return to the Mont Blanc range for the summer season, but he also felt the demands of climbing celebrity and worried that he had not yet proven himself, although few alpinists had itineraries like his. He was probably absorbed by the question of what to climb in the new year. Indeed, it was around this time that he began to make plans to complete the greatest alpine route ever climbed anywhere in the world.

On April 2, 1913, a little over a year after Paul debuted as a speaker in a smoky German beer cellar, he lectured in formal evening dress in a packed opera house in Turin. His reputation as a lecturer had spread to the general public, and less than half of the audience were mountaineers. Alpinist Ettore Canzio, who attended, said that even the non-climbers were taken by his presentation. Paul never emphasized that the difficult climbs he was talking about had been done by him and his friends. The climbers in the crowd who knew how hard his climbing really was were inevitably taken by his modesty. After the lecture, they accompanied their hero to a bar. Passing a baroque palace en route, Paul "suddenly climbed up and across a wall to the cornice traversed the roof and climbed back down again, all while still wearing his formal clothes."[212]

On April 4, Paul joined Bavarian mountaineer Willy von Bernuth at the Vittorio Emanuele II hut, near the Gran Paradiso (4061 metres) in Italy's Graian Alps. Paul had decided to try first ski ascents and descents of the Gran Paradiso and Roc di Gran Paradiso after studying photographs of the mountain taken in the summer season, which showed his good intuition for snow conditions. Seeking first ski descents was so new that few were even recorded until the 1920s. But Paul's approach to skiing had evolved.

As recently as 1912, much of his most poetic and romantic nature writing had been inspired by his long-distance ski traverses. Few of these tours were very technical, and in his articles he recalled not just the steep descents and ascents but the flora and fauna and the customs of the *Senners*. But now he sought potentially difficult first technical ascents and descents much as he sought out new rock climbs.

He and Bernuth had perfect snow and reached the summits of both peaks on April 10. The ski descent was one of the most difficult yet made in the Alps because the narrow, wooden-edged skis were hard to control at sustained speeds. High-speed turns were limited to the inefficient stem-christie or snowplow.

Paul planned to make more ski ascents, but after he skied 3540-metre-high Ciarforon, conditions deteriorated in the Graian Alps. In search of better snow, he met Walter Bing in the Bernina Alps in Switzerland. Conditions there were little better. After abandoning an attempt on Piz Roseg (3937 metres) in a storm, Paul sent his skis home and headed to Genoa for the last lecture of the season.

Genoa was in balmy Liguria, 500 kilometres south of the mountains, on the shore of the Mediterranean. Its palm trees and beaches were about as far from alpine scenery as could be imagined. Emmy Eisenberg – who saw herself as Paul's girlfriend, although Tita did not believe that their relationship was exclusive – awaited him there.

At 26, Paul had reached the average age for male marriage in Austria. Many of his contemporaries were no longer single. Paul might eventually have followed the precedent set by his father and married in his 30s, but as yet, he showed no signs of settling down. It's possible that a sense of foreboding about his climbing kept Paul from marrying because he didn't want to make a widow of a woman he loved. Yet he did not embrace or anticipate death in the mountains. The more obvious reason Paul never totally committed to a romantic relationship was not that he feared death but that he loved his independent life.

In recounting their time in Liguria, Emmy described neither romantic dinners nor visits to the beach but instead a single trip to the tourist sights of Genoa, followed by a visit to a demonstration by an Italian navy motor launch. The mountains were never far from Paul's mind. When the motor launch accelerated and the bow rose high in the water, he told Emmy that his skis had sunk into the snow on the Gran Paradiso and that wider skis, shaped like a boat hull, would ride higher in the snow. Decades later, the ski industry caught up with his idea, but Emmy did not record whether or not she found his observations a winsome addition to their holiday.

In June, Paul was back in the limestone Alps. He made the first ascent of the 1400-metre-high North Face of the Hochwanner, one of the biggest walls in the Northern Limestone Alps, and soloed two new routes on the Öfelekopf. He also soloed the first ascent of an 800-metre-long gash in the North Wall of the Mitterkaiser in the Kaisergebirge that became known as the Preuss-Schlucht. This intimidating line was geologically primal, dark, in places loose and cut so deeply into the mountain that a stream emerged from its base. Strong climbers, including Georg Leuchs, had been turned back by its difficult cracks. Paul's breathtaking solos in the limestone Alps had begun to seem inevitable.

In late June, Paul was in his apartment in Munich when Tita called him on his landlady's telephone. Tita was now a climbing celebrity working part-time as a brand ambassador for a Munich sports store. He had teamed up with Dülfer for the first ascent of Punta di Frida in the Tre Cime di Lavaredo the year before, and both he and Dülfer were now at the vanguard of modern rock technique. Tita proposed to Paul that they attempt one of the last great problems of the Bavarian Alps, the vertical, 320-metre-high South Face of the Schüsselkarspitze in the Wetterstein Alps. Tita's account provides more insight into Paul's state of mind than typically appears in the work of his more awestruck friends:

> In the spring of 1913, when we both lived in Munich, I telephoned Preuss and asked him if he wanted to come with me and try the invincible South Wall of the Schüsselkarspitze, the problem of problems at the time.

Preuss confirmed that the wall had resisted all of the attempts by German climbers. He also thought my offer was a joke in bad taste, after all our altercations. I thought my offer would stop him in his tracks, but it didn't. I wanted the best for Preuss. I knew that he had ambitions to solve the great problems, and in good faith, I would leave him all the glory and he could leave me to use all the climbing gear.

He proposed that on the wall we would adopt a system so that each of us could approach the problem according to our own style. Under these circumstances, Paolo accepted my offer willingly.

With us was Signorina Lisa Fries, the best young climber of the moment.[213] I had tried the climb twice and each time retreated with my tail between my legs. I knew the key was finding the right route, and my attempts had proven to me that the face was climbable.

We arrived at the base of the face at midday, happy, feeling strong and brimming with confidence. I led the first pitches and after about 70 metres I came up against a steep section that did not look good. As was my usual style, I climbed up to the critical point, studied it meticulously then climbed back down to my colleagues and told them it was doable, but it was very difficult. I told them I would attempt it again after a rest, but in the meantime, if Preuss wished, he could give it a try.

In fact, no guard dog would have been more ready to have a go at the pitch than Preuss, but he came back down after having a look and shared my opinion about its difficulty. I said that I would need to use rope tension to climb it, and this is where our dispute began. As I prepared the rope for our safe passage, Preuss began to climb quietly back up on his own. I hoped it wouldn't negatively affect our partnership. With difficulty, I began to climb up to set the [tension traverse] rope while I let Preuss try the pitch his way.

Preuss appeared to be stuck on the brutal wall and I asked him if he wanted a rope.

"Never," he said, "you said it was climbable," and he added that I should not interrupt his dangerous efforts.

I took offence and yelled harshly at him.

"Take the rope," I said, "and hold on tight."

He hurled insults at my ignoble person.

"I will not let you lead," he said.

I hung in his way on a tight rope, however, and blocked him, but he climbed around me with some contortionist moves. It was like a bad dream. I saw his legs tremble slightly as happens when you make great efforts. When he found the inner peace to recuperate from the great danger, he said he released Fries and I, because he had no sympathy for crazy traditional [i.e., piton-using] climbers.

Since I found myself roped up to a genuine madman, I had to take the rope and climb as I pleased. After all, I had no choice, although I had promised his mother that I would bring him home alive, and I always try to keep my word, even when it comes to trifles.

"*Servus*, Paolo!" I said, "and have a great climb."

I went back up and climbed the wall using the rope, as Preuss had refused to do. In the meantime, Preuss had changed his mind, and with a cordial handshake we were friends again. We climbed as long as the light permitted, then descended (in my case for third time) from the wall. Preuss had a lecture in Munich the next day, so a bivouac was impossible. What a disaster.[214]

The days were past when Paul's climbing partners had to return to the city for work or other responsibilities while Paul stayed on in the mountains alone. Now it was Paul's city life that precluded an unplanned bivouac and another attempt.

The same city life that could curtail his climbing plans was linked to his successes and performance in the mountains. "At risk of sounding paradoxical," he wrote, "here lies an irrefutable truth:

the higher your reputation in the sports world for the completion of a solo climb, the more the climb loses its intimate nature and its effectiveness."[215]

A climber, with or without a rope, is at their best in dangerous circumstances when they carefully weigh their true motivations. Paul had set out on dangerous, hard climbs for recognition and sport, but the attention he craved and garnered clouded his mind while he climbed.

Paul and Tita left a 70-metre fixed rope to use on an attempt they planned for the next Sunday. Tita lost his boots and descended painfully to the Wetterstein hut in his *Kletterschuhe*. That evening the trio bicycled 40 kilometres to Innsbruck, where they caught the train to Munich. Rain precluded a second attempt. Hans Fiechtl and Otto Herzog climbed the face using Tita's fixed rope soon afterwards. Paul had criticized Herzog for using half a dozen pitons on the Lalidererwand. Where Tita and Paul had been a team at odds with itself, Herzog and Fiechtl were of one mind when it came to climbing style, and their climb maintained its reputation for decades.

For Tita, the Schüsselkarspitze was the end of an era of his life heavily influenced by Paul. "On the wall [of the Schüsselkarspitze] divinely lit by the sun," he said, "on an unforgettable spring evening, I shook hands for the last time with that fantastic climber, Paolo Preuss."[216]

The story reveals a histrionic side to Paul, a dangerous devotion to his ideals on the one hand and to his reputation on the other. Tita had watched as Paul almost fell to his death. On his own, Paul could decide to climb or go down. With an audience of the beautiful Fries and his mentor, father-figure and ethical adversary, Tita, he had to go up. If Paul perceived the goal to be prestigious or if his self-image was on the line, he was willing to take greater risks than he admitted when he said that he never pushed himself to the limit.

On July 24, Paul met Ugo di Vallepiana in Courmayeur. Conditions were only slightly better than they had been when he arrived the year before, with snow well below 4000 metres. This season, however, Paul had a specific mission and no intention of limiting himself to modest climbs. Despite the weather, he and Vallepiana made straight for the Gamba hut, haunted as it was by the ghosts of Truffer and the Joneses. It would become Paul's base as he began work on a project that H.O. Jones himself might have inspired, a climb that rivalled any yet undertaken anywhere in the Alps: the 4500-metre-long Peuterey Ridge, the longest in the Alps.

The route Paul envisioned was similar to the modern Peuterey Integral, with some important variations, partly due to the state of play on the major peaks on the Peuterey itself. Paul's route would traverse the Mont Rouge de Peuterey (which is not considered part of the modern Peuterey Integral), climb the East Ridge of the normal route on the Aiguille Noire and descend its Northwest Ridge to the wide col known as the Fauteuil des Allemands (Germans' Chair). He would then climb up to and traverse the rock pillars of the Dames Anglaises, a tricky section with loose rock. The Aiguille Blanche de Peuterey above was the most serious mountaineering objective on his route. The normal route was notorious for falling rock, so Paul planned an ascent of its steep Southeast Face. He would then descend the Aiguille Blanche to the Col de Peuterey and climb to the top of Mont Blanc.

Paul planned to climb most of the peaks on the ridge separately before he enchained them in a continuous ascent. He had already been on the Mont Rouge de Peuterey, and the next peak on the ridge was the Aiguille Noire. Snow rendered the normal route up the East Ridge out of condition. Instead, he and Vallepiana made the first ascent of the 300-metre-high pillar of the Pic Gamba by the South Ridge and East Face. Although it was one of the hardest rock routes yet done in the Mont Blanc range, it was dwarfed by the mighty, unclimbed South Ridge of the Aiguille Noire de Peuterey above, which later became the crux of the Peuterey Integral.

The South Ridge was subsequently attempted unsuccessfully by many of the best climbers in the Alps, including the strong German climber Willo Welzenbach. It fell in 1930, to German climbers Karl Brendelet and Hermann Schaller, who carried bivouac gear and pitons. Vallepiana recalled Paul's assessment of the South Ridge from the summit of Pic Gamba. "'Others will climb it,'

Preuss said; 'I renounce it.' But I thought, if Paris was worth a mass, wasn't the South Ridge worth a few pitons?"[217]

Paul's statement was a polite Viennese parsing of the sentiment British climber Albert Mummery voiced in 1880, when he said that the Dent du Géant was "absolutely inaccessible by fair means." Vallepiana's belief that Paul could have climbed the South Ridge of the Aiguille Noire had he used pitons, however, was unrealistic. It would have been a giant upward step from anything yet done in the Alps. The first ascent party used aid on sections that were later free climbed at modern French 5c that Paul would have to climb free and unprotected. Friends who were not climbers of Paul's calibre sometimes unwittingly exaggerated his abilities. If Paul did not try a climb, they often assumed that he was withholding himself on account of his philosophies, rather than simply recognizing his own limitations.

Bad weather, that coda to innumerable disappointing Mont Blanc adventures, soon brought further exploration of the Peuterey Ridge to an end. Paul and Vallepiana consoled themselves with a climb on the Aiguille Rouge de Triolet and a new route on the South Ridge of Aiguille Croux. Paul also soloed a short climb on the Southeast Ridge of Punta Innominata; the first ascent of a beautiful 1000-metre rock route on the South Ridge of the Aiguille de Savoie; and the West Ridge of the Arête des Papillons. Even Paul's easier climbs were stymied by the weather. When Relly and Mina arrived in Courmayeur on August 14, Relly joined Vallepiana and Preuss for a traverse of Punta Isabella, normally a moderate outing, but bad weather forced them to retreat.

From the comfort of the Torino hut, Paul sent his mother a postcard: "I'm happy about the arrival of Mina and Tiger, but the weather is very poor. It snows above 4000 metres every night, and when the sun comes out, there is a danger of avalanches."[218] How Lina reacted to this ominous news is not recorded, but it shows how close they still were, and that he sometimes confided in his mother doubts about climbing that he hid from his partners.

Italian guide and top climber Angelo Dibona was at the Torino, waiting for conditions to improve so that he could take a client up the Grépon. Although Dibona had been singled out by Paul for his use of pitons, he and Paul became friends on this, their first meeting. "I only met Preuss three times in the mountains," said Dibona. "He was a mountaineer and a fine man, with no sense of superiority towards anyone. I have never felt more satisfaction than I did speaking to him in the mountains. On the question of aids we agreed, but being an alpine guide, I sometimes use them and in particular, on walls of a technical nature and some problems in the Mont Blanc range. [Preuss] had a simple, solitary nature."[219]

Dibona and Paul bonded quickly partly because of a code of male friendship that had developed among alpinists. In the mountains, the last outpost of wildness in Europe, men believed that they could be more straightforward than in the city, and a premium was put on comradeship based not on propriety or pride but on shared emotions.[220] As Lammer said, the mountains were a haven for those who rejected the airs of civility in favour of emotional directness and sincerity.

In this manly communality of spirit, a new, all but unspoken consensus had emerged that Paul had correctly identified the core values of climbing, and had done the community a service by sticking to them. Even piton users like Dibona appreciated that Paul had drawn a distinction between their use and abuse. In a sense, his devotion to his ideals justified the compromises of other climbers by proving that at least one man could recognize the ideal at the heart of the sport. As Paul began to accept that few climbers would adopt his methods, he began to speak of himself as destined to renounce them. He came to see his style as a narrow path that was not for everyone. Among the common climbers who used technological aids, his approach became legendary.

Paul gave up on the Italian side for the time being and searched for better conditions near the Requin Refuge. His next objective, the Dent du Géant, was a leaning, 350-metre tooth of granite, and a lodestone for stylistic controversies.

English climber Albert Mummery had attempted the first ascent from the southwest side with Swiss guide Alexander Burgener in 1880. They were turned back by the section which later became known as the Burgener Slabs. Mummery's pronouncement that the peak was "absolutely inaccessible by fair means" was later vindicated by the style of the first ascent. Chamonix guide Jean Charlet-Straton had come within ten metres of the summit on a solo attempt in 1876, famously comparing the peak afterwards to "a great lady who chooses to remain a virgin, perhaps for the best." In 1882, Italian guide Jean-Joseph Maquignaz, along with his son Baptiste and nephew Daniel, climbed to within a few metres of the summit after a four-day siege with the aid of metal pegs hammered into the rock to anchor fixed ropes. The Alpine Club in London was apoplectic and accused the Maquignazes of using explosives to make their climb. The party was proud of its achievement, however, and carved the letter M in the rock near the summit to commemorate it. The climb still sports fixed ropes today.

In 1900, Thomas Maischberger, Heinrich Pfannl and Franz Zimmer made a bold free route to the summit via the North Ridge. The Dent du Géant's South Face remained a free climbing challenge. Without using the fixed ropes, the Burgener Slabs and the steep dihedral above were almost as hard as the most difficult climbs in the Mont Blanc range. The peak was the last major named summit in the range to fall but also the first to be gained by largely artificial means. Its beauty and history made it a perfect objective on which Paul could prove the validity of his style.

Weather forecasts were primitive, so climbers were forced to rely on lore and educated guesswork and gamble that any good weather would last long enough to complete their climb. At the first break in the weather, Paul hoped for the best and made his way up the long access slabs and gullies of the Dent du Géant. It started to snow, and the winds picked up as he climbed higher. In dry conditions, soloing the Burgener Slabs would have taxed Paul's abilities. Climbing the same rock covered in snow, he would have been at the limit of his abilities; a fatal slip would have awaited him on almost every move. As he clung to the tiny, rocky summit, one of the smallest in the Mont Blanc range, the storm became even more intense.

Modern climbers descend by abseiling the exposed south side of the peak. Climbers in 1913 descended the Southwest Face itself. It was a difficult proposition in good weather, involving abseils, downclimbing and shinnying down the fixed ropes. The storm would have qualified as an emergency condition in which Paul would allow abseiling or other aids, like the fixed ropes. Since Paul recorded no such compromises, it must be surmised that he solo downclimbed one of the hardest routes in the Mont Blanc range in a snowstorm.

The experience would have built up Paul's confidence that, when necessary, he could escape hard alpine routes in terrible conditions without resorting to aids, but it also took a toll on him. The postcard he sent Lina on August 12, the day after the Dent du Géant, revealed his mental state: "Horrible time yesterday. I'm done. Leaving for Florence and Genoa."[221]

Genoa still held no interest for Paul, and likewise, despite the company of Relly and Mina, the Renaissance churches of Florence soon bored him. When Relly and Mina took the train for Venice, he returned to the Alps and, for once, found Mont Blanc under blue skies.

Paul returned to his Peuterey Ridge project without delay. His first objective was the Aiguille Noire de Peuterey, but even the normal route on the South Wall and East Ridge had a reputation for being long and complicated. None of Paul's friends in Courmayeur wanted to join him on the ascent. Paul declared that he would solo the climb and wave his shirt on the summit to prove it. According to Aldo Bonacossa, Paul "left his bivouac on the Fauteuil des Allemands at 5 a.m., and we thought he would not arrive on the summit before midday… In fact, it was a beautiful day, and at 10 a.m., something white appeared on the summit…. at 4:30, he was drinking coffee with us in Courmayeur, none the worse for his experience."[222]

Paul's last Mont Blanc range climb of the summer was his greatest alpine climb and most important first ascent in the range. The beautiful Aiguille Blanche de Peuterey (4112 metres) was rarely climbed. All three routes to the summit had a reputation for rockfall and the mountain was exposed to strong west winds. None of the routes were easily accessible from Paul's planned bivouac on the Brèche des Dames Anglaises.

Bonacossa and his climbing partner, Carlo Prochownick, agreed to attempt Paul's proposed line up the Southeast Ridge, which promised to be difficult but less exposed to falling rock than the existing routes. After waiting for a couple of clear days to set the snow, the trio climbed the Brenva glacier to the Dames Anglaises. The weather was unstable the next day, so they made an abortive attempt on a new route on the Dames Anglaises while they waited it out.

After a cold bivouac, they set out at dawn on firm snow under a clear, deep blue sky. Paul had learned new ice techniques from Eckenstein and was armed with modern crampons and a shortened ice axe. Bonacossa was impressed by the grace and speed with which Paul climbed and by the fact that he never stopped to chop steps. The crux was hard mixed climbing in a chimney and a difficult traverse to the Northeast Ridge, all led by Paul. Before lightweight stoves, bivy bags and high-tech shell gear, an open bivouac in the high mountains could be deadly, so they made the climb and descent in a continuous 28-hour push.

In the usually restrained pages of British *Alpine Journal*, Günther von Saar later gushed about the route, saying that Paul "succeeded in solving a magnificent problem: the ascent of the Aiguille Blanche de Pétéret [*sic*] by the S.E. ridge, and traverse to the N.E., so that he discovered a way, difficult it is true, but quite safe from falling stones, up this beautiful and formidable mountain."[223]

Paul had reconnoitred the Aiguilles Rouge, Noire and Blanche de Peuterey and the Dames Anglaises. He was in a good position to complete his project because the ridge offered few difficulties between the Aiguille Blanche and the summit. On August 28, Paul wrote to his mother on a postcard with an illustration of the Aiguille Blanche de Peuterey: "I have climbed the first ascent of the beautiful Southeast Ridge of the Aiguille Blanche. If the weather stays beautiful, I will stay a few days more. Your Old Pauli."[224]

It was late in the season, however, and the weather turned worse. Paul never returned to his project. In 1934, Adolf Göttner, Ludwig Schmaderer and Ferdinand Krobath made the first ascent of the modern version of the Peuterey traverse, the Integral, which skipped the Mont Rouge de Peuterey but included the South Ridge of the Aiguille Noire. Paul returned to Altaussee, where he wrote Emmy Eisenberg, who was convalescing from an injured knee in Vienna.

Dear Emmy,

Thank you for the postcard. The weather is poor and I am not climbing, so don't feel sad. We will wait for October when maybe we can make some climbs together. I will stay here in the hopes that [Friedrich] Henning and R. [Rudi] Redlich will come to see me. The weather is so very bad. Around the 20th I will come to Vienna. I finally made a good climb in Courmayeur, the South Ridge of the Aiguille Blanche, first ascent. A thousand greetings from your old Paul.[225]

The card picture was the Trisselwand rising above the Aussee, one of the peaks they might well climb together. On September 20, Paul went to Vienna to give the first presentation of the lecture season to the Austrian Ski Club. Before he left, he had begun an itinerary program of climbing aggressive new routes in the Dachstein and Totes Gebirge. Redlich and Henning were at the forefront of rock climbing and Redlich was also a photographer. Together with Paul they would have formed an ideal team for hard climbing and collecting new photographs for presentations as long as the season held out.

The need to come up with news and material for lectures added a professional justification for Paul's lifelong reluctance to call an end to a route, a weekend or a climbing season. Clear autumn skies over Styria, a second trying summer in the Western Alps and the impending lecture season gave him all the inspiration he needed to surrender to his carefree alpine *flâneur*'s inclination and delay calling off the 1913 season as long as possible.

Valhalla: Mandlkogel North Face, October 1913

Shall we try it tomorrow?

—Paul Preuss

Redlich and Henning cancelled, so Paul convinced his friend Günther von Saar, a medical professor from Innsbruck, to spend the week climbing with him. Saar's impressive record included the North Face of the Hochtor in the Gesäuse and the first ascent of the pinnacle of the Campanile di Val Montanaia. He was, however, eight years older than Paul, with most of his hardest climbing behind him, and he was also less ambitious than Paul or, for that matter, Redlich and Henning.

Together with Saar, Paul took advantage of the beautiful weather and made a number of ascents in the Gosaukamm and neighbouring groups. But when Paul suggested making the first ascent of the East Face of the Strichkogel, Saar demurred. Instead of choosing another climb, Paul soloed it.

On September 15, they were caught out in a thunderstorm while descending from the Gross Donnerkogel and made for the weathered Zwieselalm hut. There they found Hans Reinl, whose 1906 first ascent of the West Face of the Trisselwand with Karl Greenitz and Franz Kleinhans had introduced modern rock climbing to the Totes Gebirge. Reinl was in the area to research his upcoming Totes Gebirge guidebook.

The next evening, Paul, Reinl and Saar sat outside the hut. It is easy to imagine Reinl and Saar's impression of Paul just from the photographs. Here was a man on a victory lap after a season on the hardest climbs in Europe; a man who had made his first unroped climb at the age of 13, who climbed hundreds of routes every year, whose life was the mountains. Even his clothes, in the ancient local style, expressed his relationship to his environment. Reinl, the greatest authority on the Gosaukamm, pointed out an unclimbed rock ridge in a ceremonial gesture of respect for Paul. Saar described the scene:

> straight in front of us the N. [North] face of the Mandlko-gel pierced threatening and ghostly into the clear evening sky. "This face is the finest problem in the Gosaukamm!" exclaimed Preuss, and at once became absorbed in study-ing, with the help of his glass, the details of this formid-able wall. "Over 150 metres high, Schrofensockel [pillar] up to the Plattenschuss [slab]; then ascending traverse to the right up to the ridge where the N. face and the W. face join; up this ridge which is about 200 metres in height and pitched at an angle of 80 degrees; at the top of it, traverse to the left to the short cleft which terminates between the two summit teeth. Shall we try it to-morrow [sic]?" We others doubted the possibility of this climb; Preuss hoped that the very slabby rock was firm every-where. We declined the expedition, on the grounds that we could not secure each other effectively with the rope; good, then he would attempt it alone a fortnight later, for he certainly intended to try the finest problem of the whole Gosaukamm that season.[226]

Saar and Reinl had little reason to fear for Paul's life simply be-cause he planned to climb the Mandlkogel; his solos had become commonplace. A few days later, they watched him empty his ruck-sack below the unclimbed East Wall of the Wasserkarturm and change into his *Kletterschuhe* with workmanlike nonchalance. Saar wrote:

> before we even realized it, we saw a blond head appear on the rocks above, heard some loose rock fall, and then a feline figure snaked up the vertical wall, both masterful and elegant on chimneys and slabs that looked impos-sible. Higher up, it got harder, and we held our breath as we followed that agile figure crawling up the grey stone with regular and safe rhythm. And then we saw the ele-gant figure standing on top. In one hour, he had made the

first ascent of the East Wall of the Wasserkarturm.... Before a half hour had passed, our friend came around the bottom of the cliff, and said, simply: "A little harder than the Cima Piccola di Lavaredo [in the Dolomites]." [227]

On September 18, the party broke up and Paul travelled to Vienna to make a presentation to the Austrian Ski Club. The skiers were anxious to hear Paul speak on his latest cause: opposition to a proposed ban of professional ski instructors from ski competitions. In an article in Schmidkunz's *Winter* magazine, Paul had decried the ban because it artificially lowered the standard of competition. His original antipathy towards instructors of mountain sports, based on his zealous youthful reading of guideless climbing literature, had evolved into a real concern for their well-being.

If Paul saw his mother, his uncle Sigmund or Emmy in Vienna, he kept his visits short. On September 21, the day after the lecture, Paul returned to Altaussee to resume climbing. It had been a long season and he had driven himself through a string of rigorous efforts with few rests, and his immune system finally rebelled. In Altaussee, he came down with a fever and a sore throat he had picked up in Vienna, the city to which the Preuss men had never developed an immunity. Paul was usually stoic in the face of sickness or injury, and his lifelong skepticism of medical advice had not abated. The knowledge that a throat infection had killed his father, however, must have played a role in his decision to call the village doctor.

His condition turned out to be potentially serious. The doctor identified Paul's chest pain, fatigue, shortness of breath and dizziness as symptomatic of angina. He prescribed eight days' rest in bed. After four days, when the fever began to break, Paul decided he was cured. Lina was in Vienna, and the housekeeper knew better than to try to discourage him from packing his climbing gear. On September 28, he left 53 Puchen on his bicycle for the Zwieselalm hut, doubtless already having in mind the North Face of the Mandlkogel, "the finest problem in the Gosaukamm." He told the housekeeper that he would be back by October 8.

Yet Paul must have felt a little unsure of himself. Instead of taking advantage of the good weather that had been so rare that season and proceeding directly to the Mandlkogel, he teamed up with local climber Anton Steinmaier. Together, roped, they climbed the 550-metre Northeast Ridge of the Freyaturm before Paul took on his first solo since his illness, the North Face of the Schafkogel.

On October 2, Paul joined in a season's-end celebration with Steinmaier and some other climbers at the Zwieselalm hut. The custodian, Elisabetta Steiner, recalled that the climbers sang, drank and toasted each other and the mountains until late into the evening.[228]

But the season had not quite ended for Paul. The weather was still good the next morning, when Steinmaier and the others departed. Paul might well have decided to go with them and begin writing up the year's adventures. Instead, he stayed to climb by himself. He asked Steiner, who was preparing to close up for the season, for the key to the little Scharwand hut on the Vorderer Gosausee, the lake beneath the North Face of the Mandlkogel.

Paul hiked up on his own and spent the night in the Scharwand hut, where he would have remembered the scene before him from the wedding-present painting that hung on his parents' bedroom wall. He would have spent some time inspecting the route from there with his telescope, using his knowledge of the differences in coloration, texture and angle of the rock to guess where the difficulties would be greatest.

He also would have kept a close eye on the changing sky. Clouds were coming in from the northwest, and the wind was picking up. But only that summer, Paul had survived his solo of the Dent du Géant – a climb almost as committing, if better known and slightly less steep than the Mandlkogel – in a storm, even if he had told Lina it was a terrible experience.

Few climbers were as thoughtful as Paul, and in the silence of the alpine night, he would have had time to contemplate his philosophies. Few climbers had such well-developed soloing skills and general climbing technique. He had first begun to chart the moral and psychological ranges of climbing *allein* as a boy, and moved on to the Planspitze, the Totenkirchl, the Campanile Basso, the Mitterkaiser and hundreds of other climbs, including the first ascent of the East Wall of the Wasserkarturm just a few days before. Paul admitted that he sometimes struggled to concentrate while soloing, but the main themes in his written reflections on soloing were self-confidence and reward.

"Wherever there are no purely objective present dangers," he wrote, "I am a solid solo climber. I know how deep a friendship there is between two climbers, and I willingly admit that the danger is doubled when one climbs alone, but all this is compensated a thousand-fold by the pleasure one feels while soloing. The colossal power of nature, the most intimate emotions of our heart, the subtlest games of our thoughts offer us the most joyous moments when, in the heights covered in sunshine, we wage, all alone, a joyous combat for victory."[229]

At first light, Paul hiked to the North Face and picked his way up the lower-angled ramp of suspect rock that led to the skyline of the Mandlkogel's North Ridge. Average temperatures in the sun at that altitude in October would have been close to the freezing mark. The steep main ridge was in the shade, and the clouds dimmed the sunlight and portended bad weather. The cold would make it harder to grasp holds securely; that, together with the possibility of snow later in the day, comprised just the sort of "objective present danger" that Paul had admitted as a valid reason not to solo, but he continued nonetheless.

The rock of the Mandlkogel was as dubious as Saar had predicted it would be. This would have slowed Paul down as he tested every hold and sometimes climbed down or traversed to avoid loose or overly difficult unstable rock. It would also have made the race against the weather more stressful. After 300 metres of hard climbing, however, Paul reached a point about 100 metres below the summit.

Paul was known to extend his climbing plans either to wait out poor weather or to take advantage of a fine spell to add a few more summits to his trip. In the days before hut telephones, mountaineers' loved ones had no choice but to hope for the best when climbers were delayed. On October 10, however, the housekeeper at 53 Puchen became concerned. Elisabetta Steiner was contacted, but she had already closed the Zwieselalm hut for the season and had last seen Paul when he borrowed the key to the Scharwand hut.

Emmy Eisenberg was in Vienna and expected an overdue message from Paul to confirm their climbing plans. She called Mina and Relly, who were vacationing in Altaussee. It was unlike Paul not to follow up on climbing plans. The housekeeper told Relly that Paul had set out for the Zwieselalm hut. There, in the hut logbook, Relly found the last entry in Paul's handwriting: the North Ridge of the Mandlkogel, *allein*.

Relly and a local guide organized a rescue team. News spread quickly through the climbing community, and many of Paul's friends rushed to Altaussee to help with the rescue. Hans Dülfer came down from Kufstein. Alexander Hartwich came from Vienna. Local climbers who had put their boots and ice axes away for the season returned to the mountains without a thought of the cold and snow, to join in the rescue of the great Paul Preuss.

The weather had become even worse, and new snow made it a desperate task to break the avalanche-prone trail to the Scharwand hut. Paul might still have been alive but trapped somewhere by snow; on the other hand, the snow increased the possibility that he had perished in a frozen bivouac or an avalanche.

On October 14, on the ramp at the base of the Mandlkogel, the rescuers probed the snow with their ice axes and found Paul's body a metre below the surface. His injuries were described as grievous and consistent with a great fall. His face, however, with its high cheekbones, big eyelids and characteristic subtle grin, was uninjured and serene.

The rescuers found a small appointment book with his lecture dates in his jacket pocket, a reminder of the relationship between Paul's goals as a climber and his reputation. In his back pocket, they found a whistle like the one his father had given him to blow if he was lost and needed help. It was crushed by the impact of the fall.[230]

The rescuers, now pall bearers, descended to treeline and cut fir branches for a makeshift bier. The whole team was deeply affected by the task of bringing the greatest climber Austria had ever seen back down to the valley. As they drew the body behind them to the Zwieselalm hut on the boughs from the forests in which Paul had played as a boy, Dülfer wept.

FROM TOP:

The Campanile Basso.
PRINT BY ADALBERT HOLZER

Otto Herzog on the
Dreikinzenspitze.

Abseiling was safer than traditional roped downclimbing shown here, but many, like Paul Preuss, considered it dubious style, or even cheating.

ILLUSTRATION: ERNST ENZENSPERGER

Munich's Georg
Winkler, the model for
a generation of extreme
climbers.

Paul Preuss,
Gymnasium student.

FROM TOP:

Alpine Catholicism. The guides' morning prayer on the Grossglockner.
PAINTING BY OTTO BARTH

Munich's Otto "Rambo" Herzog, introduced the karabiner that revolutionized ropework.

Paul Preuss's reconnaissance of the East Face of the Campanile Basso.

Paul Preuss on the North Face of the Hochtor in the Gesäuse in September, 1911.

Paul Preuss, 1912.
PHOTO: ALBERT ASELS

Predigtstuhl

Anton Karg phot.   Stripsenjochhaus (1580 m, Sektion Kufstein) im Kaisergebirge

The Stripsenjochhaus hut, a centre of hard rock climbing in the Alps.

Hans Dülfer, Paul Preuss's sometime climbing partner, and
Hanne Franz.

FROM TOP:

Tita Piaz, Devil of the Dolomites, was haunted by Paul's Ghost.

The Reverend Friedrich Selle, Protestant pastor of Altaussee, botanist and nature enthusiast.

The team that conquered the West Face of the Totenkirchl in 1908 at photo night for the Kufstein Section. Left to right, Rudolf Schietzold, Josef Klammer, Tita Piaz, Franz Schroffenegger.

PHOTO: ANTON KARG

Paul Preuss, climber and lecturer, in his study at 92 Adalbertstrasse, Munich, in 1912.
PHOTO: UGO DI VALLEPIANA

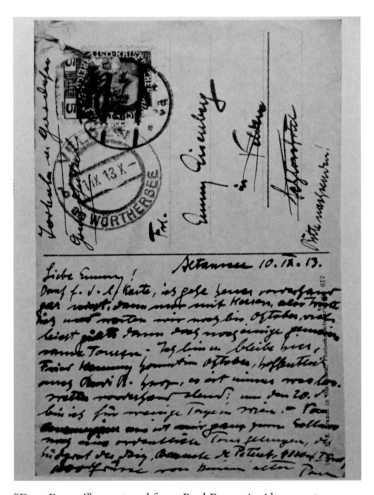

"Dear Emmy!" a postcard from Paul Preuss in Altaussee to
Emmy Eisenberg in Vienna, written shortly before his death.

The North Ridge of the Mandlkogel where Paul died.
PHOTO: SEVERINO CASARA

FROM TOP:

Paul Preuss, foreground, and Hans Reinl at the Zweiselealm hut, on the night they discussed the North Ridge of the Mandlkogel, a month before he died.
PHOTO: GÜNTHER VON SAAR

Paul Preuss with his bicycle, on a sunny fall day in 1913.
PHOTO: GÜNTHER VON SAAR

Paul Preuss on the difficult Schiefen Reiss on the Totenkirchl.
PHOTO: WALTER SCHMIDKUNZ

Paul Preuss in front of the West Face of the Totenkirchl, which he
soloed in 1911.

Paul Preuss and his sister Mina on the Campanile Basso in the
Dolomites, 1911.
PHOTO: PAUL RELLY

Paul Relly on the Campanile Basso.
PHOTO: PAUL PREUSS

Left to right, Paul Preuss, girlfriend Emmy Eisenberg, and Walter Schmidkunz, publisher of the *German Alpine Times* in Selva di Val Gardena in the Dolomites, August, 1911.

PHOTO: PAUL REDLICH

Paul Preuss on the delicate Matejak Traverse on the North Ridge of the Predigtstuhl in June, 1911.

PHOTO: WALTER SCHMIDKUNZ

FROM TOP:

Paul Preuss and college
friend Walter Bing making
climbing plans at the Café
Stefanie in Munich, 1912.
PAINTING BY HANS LASSER

Hans Fiechtl's fixed
eyelet pitons, along with
karabiners, led to the
proliferation and popularity
of fixed pitons.

CLOCKWISE FROM TOP LEFT:

Franz Nieberl, the "Pope of the Kaiser Range," penned one of the most scathing critiques of Paul's climbing ethics.

The karabiner transformed the use of pitons by making it simple and secure.
ILLUSTRATION: ERNST PLATZ

Paul's friend Tita Piaz had used combined tactics like this on the West Face of the Totenkirchl. Paul spoke against the prevailing opinion that they were free climbing.
ILLUSTRATION: CARL MOOS

Paul Preuss's biographer, Severino Casara, left, relied heavily on Paul's former girlfriend, Emmy Eisenberg, centre, whose leg is still bothering her more than ten years after it stopped her from climbing with Paul in 1913. On the right is Italian rock climbing star Emilio Comici.

Valkyries offer a crown to Georg Winkler, the teenage conqueror of the Winkler Tower (seen in the background), on the cover of his posthumously published diary.

Anglo-German painter E.T. Compton was one of Paul's climbing partners. He painted this stunning picture of the Vajolet Towers when they were a testing ground for hard rock climbing. Left to right, the Delago Tower, the Piaz Tower below, the Stabeler Tower and the Winkler Tower.

Anna Freud, the daughter of Sigmund Freud, was one of Paul Preuss's climbing partners.

A postcard of the Stripsenjochhaus. The Totenkirchl rises behind.

The climber as "a feast for the ravens."
ILLUSTRATION: ANTON SCHONECKER

Emil Zsigmondy, whose picture hung next to Georg Winkler's on Paul's wall. A champion of climbing ethics and guideless climbing, Zsigmondy died on the Meije in 1885.

With little or no protection, a leader fall could tear the whole party off the mountain. Paul argued it was safer to go unroped.
ILLUSTRATION: OTTO BARTH

Traunsee and the Traunstein, climbed by Paul Preuss's mother, Lina, when she was a governess at Schloss Ebenzweier

Hohe Wand 1135 m.
Kletterpartie am Kanzelriss

CLOCKWISE FROM TOP:

A simple picture belies a dangerous technique that limited the popularity of pitons. To use the ring piton the leader had to untie from the rope, thread it through the ring and tie in again.
ILLUSTRATION: CARL MOOS

A postcard of rock climbing at the Hohe Wand in Peilstein in the Vienna Hausbergen.

The Dent du Géant in the Mont Blanc range. Alfred Mummery once considered it "impossible by fair means." Paul soloed it in a snowstorm.

CLOCKWISE FROM TOP LEFT:

Paul Preuss and Munich college friend Walter Bing on a ski trip.

Johannes Brahms, director of the Vienna Conservatory when Eduard Preuss taught there.

Austrian Colonel Georg Bilgeri, whose books and modern ski binding popularized skiing in Austria.

Paul Preuss on the North Ridge of the Predigtstuhl.
PHOTO: WALTER SCHMIDKUNZ

Lina Lauchheim's hometown, Strasbourg, destroyed by German artillery, 1870.

Otto Herzog, shirtless, on the right, on the Western Front.

CLOCKWISE FROM TOP LEFT:

The Evangelical church on the Dorotheergasse in Vienna, where Paul Preuss became a Christian.

ILLUSTRATION: ERWIN PENDL

The University of Vienna, ca. 1880.

The Propylaea in Munich, a popular bouldering objective of Paul Preuss and Hans Dülfer.

ILLUSTRATION: LEO VON KLENZE

Dangerous hobbies like duelling were popular with students of the University of Vienna in the 1900s. Mountaineering offered an even more dangerous thrill for accomplished duellists like Martin Freud.

Auf die Mensur, fertig, los!

CLOCKWISE FROM TOP LEFT:

The Preuss memorial, Altaussee, Austria.
PHOTO: WIKIMEDIA COMMONS

Paul Preuss's hammer and pitons in the Messner Museum in Corones, Italy.
PHOTO: WIKIMEDIA COMMONS

The Bischofsmütze, which Paul and a friend soloed when he was fourteen.

Ring piton and picture hook piton. Both had serious liabilities.
ILLUSTRATION: CARL MOOS

Ringhaken

sog. Mizzi Langer- haken

Free-soloists overcome basophobia, the fear of falling that is wired into the animal brain, so completely that they startle and fascinate the average climber. More than a few, however, have paid for their feats with their lives.[231] When they do fall, their demise is often blamed on anything but their choice to solo: relationship stress, society's pressure to conform, the weather or, most intriguingly, the bonds of destiny that tie them to the highest and purest laws of climbing.

Some free-soloists have had their climbs filmed. In some instances, the filmmakers could not bear to watch through their cameras, for fear that they would witness their subject's death. Sometimes, instead of refusing to record what they could not watch, they deployed automatic cameras, which have the moral advantage of indifference to the plight of the climber. The moment on the wall that leads to the death of a solitary, unroped climber remains so intensely private that it has not been recorded. The actual reasons why soloists fall and die remain matters of myth and speculation.

Naturally, many wanted to know how Paul, one of the best climbers in the world, fell from the Mandlkogel after succeeding on well over 1,000 other climbs. The vacuum was filled with explanations and myths, the most prevalent of which might be called the knife theory. Modern solo climber Alex Honnold summarizes it: "I can just picture it. Preuss stops for a lunch break. He takes out his knife, maybe to cut an apple or a hunk of cheese. The knife slips out of his hand, so he lunges forward to grab it, forgetting for an instant where he is. Goes off the edge, tries to grab something, and misses. Talk about the worst four seconds of his life!"[232]

The knife theory, however, originated with the first party to climb the North Ridge of the Mandlkogel, not the rescue party, and in the original version of the story, Paul dropped the knife while cutting rappel slings rather than enjoying a picnic.

In September 1923, Erwin Hein and Karl Schreiner saw the North Ridge of the Mandlkogel from the Wasserkarturm and decided to attempt it. In 1971, Gosaukamm expert Willi von End wrote an extensive article on climbing on the Mandlkogel and reported on Hein and Schreiner's first complete ascent of the North Ridge. "Suddenly," he quotes Hein saying, "'our gaze fell on the

Mandlkogel North Ridge, falling down hundreds of metres into a wild gorge… our desire to climb this unbelievably bold line became overwhelming." On September 8, 1923, Hein and Schreiner climbed the ramp to the base of the ridge. There, said Hein, "we stood speechless before this wonder of nature and admired the view.… During the lower part of the climb, I saw an open, already quite rusty pocket knife and soon we came upon a rotten rucksack full of rope slings. In my mind, I saw a lonely mountaineer high up on a narrow, dizzying ridge, cutting a sling. Suddenly, he drops the knife and he bends down and falls off the steep wall. It must be assumed, according to this fact [i.e., the location of the knife relative to the wall above] that Preuss had already overcome most of the difficulties."[233]

Paul carried a rope over his shoulder on the East Face of the Campanile Basso, presumably in case he needed to call off the climb and retreat. It was a safeguard he must have employed elsewhere. Paul's only option when he could not downclimb was to abseil. Photos of Paul abseiling at Klettergärten for presentations on rope work show how well he understood the technique. He was a meticulous planner and technician and would have cut the slings Hein and Schreiner found in the pack before he started climbing rather than leave the task until an emergency forced him to abseil.

The knife could have been dropped already open for a variety of reasons, or been flicked open by the impact of striking the rock after it slipped out of a pocket or a rucksack; there is no evidence that the knife played a part in Paul's death. If he did drop it, he would likely have let it go rather than forgotten where he was so completely that he lunged for it and fell.

The discovery of a cairn, or Steinmann, on the ridge high above the location of the knife corroborated the idea that Preuss took a break in which he might have had time to use the knife and drop it. He had left a small cairn in an alcove on the Campanile Basso and three on the top of the North Face of the Ödstein as evidence of his first ascents. If he had planned to retreat from the Mandlkogel, he might have left one to mark his high point. The two caveats to the cairn theory are that the first reference to a pile of stones at Paul's assumed high point is in a 1914 obituary, written nine years before anyone had climbed on the ridge above the approach ramp,[234] and Schreiner and Hein, who found the knife and the pack, do not mention any cairns.

The most obvious reason for the accident is the difficulty of the climb itself. In the words of Willi von End:

> the [route's] spell of immortality was not disturbed for another ten years [after Paul's death], and thus it remained the most beautiful [unclimbed] problem in the Gosaukamm... The first attempt [after Paul's] was by Karl Hermüller and Ludwig Böttcher in 1922. On August 8 they had made the first ascent of the North Face of the Wasserkarturm. On August 11, with Fritz Bechtold and Willi Merkl, they made the fifth ascent of the Däumling, and Bechthold and Merkl discouraged them [from trying the North Ridge of the Mandlkogel]. Böttcher writes: "We might have climbed the North Ridge of the Mandlkogel, if not for Bechtold and Merkl, whose successes in the Wilder Kaiser convinced us that they were better climbers than us, and they had declared the ridge unclimbable."[235]

Merkl, it should be noted, was one of the best climbers in the world at the time.

Even a 1996 guidebook cautions climbers against taking the North Ridge lightly: "An example of the fact that highly acclaimed routes do not have to be the best, the climb offers all of the alpine challenges: a long, complex approach, brittle rock, questionable pitons and a complicated descent. Nonetheless, it's a very beautiful line with a great reputation. Nobody, however, should say they were not warned."[236]

The storm that buried Paul's body beneath a metre and a half of snow undoubtedly played a role in the tragedy. It is impossible to know exactly how poor conditions were on the Mandlkogel, but Casara believed that the winds could have been strong enough to blow Paul off as he climbed.[237] Completing the North Ridge of the Mandlkogel would have been a challenge of an even higher order than the Dent du Géant, but Paul would have had a better chance of completing the climb than waiting out a stormy bivouac. The Eastern Alps now have a comparatively benign reputation when it comes to the risk of death by hypothermia, but in 1913, storms could and did kill climbers there.

Paul had nothing to keep him warm but his jacket, and he knew that finishing the climb offered him the best chance of survival. If he did choose to descend the difficult, snowy rock he had completed, the risk of a slip was higher than it would have been climbing upwards. Since ropes were usually about 30 metres long, abseils were limited to 15 metres. Even if he could have found enough natural rock anchors for a dozen abseil slings (for he carried no pitons), twice as many as most climbers carried, he would have to downclimb substantial sections of the route to make it to the safety of the ramp.

Paul was also still sick. According to the doctor, he was still supposed to be in bed, recovering from his throat infection and attack of angina. One of the symptoms was dizziness. In his weakened state, he had climbed a new route on the Freyaturm and soloed the Schafkogel before finding himself on a major new route in a snowstorm.

Free-soloists sometimes die on sunny days on climbs well beneath their abilities, because the margin for error is so narrow. American soloist John Bachar, one of the greatest rock climbers of all time, fell to his death from a moderate climb near Mammoth Lakes, California, on a fine July day in 2009. Paul died attempting a difficult, isolated, unclimbed alpine rock route in poor weather. The best climbers of Paul's time assessed his situation to have been dire even if he'd had a partner. Consider these words from the 1913–14 yearbook of the Alpen-Klub Hoch Glück in Munich:

> The dreadful, steep North Face of the Mandlkogel evoked horror even in most mountain-hardened eyes. But Preuss always trusted his own strength, and knew no fear on the rock, for it was the most beautiful problem in the Gosaukamm. He stood, then looked again at the route which was to lead him to the summit, and behind him was grinning death, but he neither knew nor

felt his presence. "Fear and anxiety I have never felt," he once remarked, "it is only interest and excitement that accompany me on a new journey of joy." He went on to the work, already enjoying in his animated spirit the difficulties which will oppose him, and from time to time, he built a cairn. The lower wall gave him an opportunity to try out his phenomenal ability, and then came something which hindered him. The sluggish body failed to obey the exultant spirit and fell down into the precipitous depth, but the spirit parted and flew up to Walhall. A few stones rolled down into the ravine, and then it was quiet. He lay there, who once could confidently feel himself king in the realm of the mountains, crushed and mutilated, his life lost, far from his friends.[238]

Up until a few months after Paul's death, Valhalla, the abode of the spirits of warriors who fell on the battlefield in acts of bravery, had been an obscure, *völkisch* term reserved for operas and the neo-pagan fringe. As the political crises in Europe mounted, as armies mustered and war seemed inevitable, nationalists promised Valhalla to every young volunteer who died a hero.

Although as far as the Hoch Glück was concerned, Paul Preuss, despite being born a Jew, was admitted into Valhalla, the Catholic priest of Altaussee protested against burying a Jew and a Protestant in the village cemetery. Eventually, however, the Preuss family's connections in the village and beyond, and Paul's fame and popularity, convinced the priest to allow the family a small, dark plot next to the mortuary.

On a grey autumn day, Lina, Sophie, Emmy, Alexander Hartwich, Paul Relly, Uncle Sigmund, Tita Piaz, some 50 climbers and scores of *Senners* followed the hearse from the Evangelical church to the cemetery. Dülfer continued to weep. Mina said that her brother's death was more devastating to her than even her father's had been, and that those who witnessed the funeral would never forget it. Paul's climbing partner Günther von Saar said, "[Paul] now rests from his bold expeditions and his bold conceptions in the quiet cemetery of Aussee."[239]

The inscription carved on Paul's handsome marble headstone reads: "Here lies Dr. Paul Preuss born in Altaussee on 19 August, 1886, died in the Gosauer mountains on 3 Oct. 1913."

Unlike his father, whose remains were tucked away in the Jewish quarter of the sprawling Vienna Zentralfriedhof, Paul was buried in Catholic hallowed ground, in the midst of his Styrian mountains and commemorated by one of the finest memorials in the cemetery. At Eduard's funeral, his uncles and the rabbi had recited the Kaddish, a song of Israel's hope for the future. At Paul's, the mourners would have sung Martin Luther's sombre "Ein feste Burg ist unser Gott" (a mighty fortress is our God), a hymn redolent with the dual imagery of heaven as both a city and a mountain. Paul joined his hero Georg Winkler and the throng of young ghosts that haunt the annals of mountaineering, mourned not only by a small cortège of family members but by the *Senners* of Altaussee and climbers throughout Europe.

The Sleeper of Altaussee

You have conquered yourself, but why are you only showing me yourself as a victim? I want to see you as the conqueror. Cast roses into the abyss and say, "Here is my tribute to the beast that did not know how to devour me."
—Friedrich Nietzsche

Paul's restless drive and vision of life did not leave the world as suddenly as he did. His memory haunted friends like ·Alexander Hartwich. "I was a friend in his teens," Hartwich said, "when the human heart is still able to open up... In long night talks, wandering through the dewy lakes of Altaussee, the air was still and cool, the starry sky arched high, and spun peacefully, we were close to each other, and those things bonded us more firmly than the rock and the rope.... as I write this, it seems to me as if a narrow shadow were moving across the room, reminding the dead what he was like in life, a tuft of fine, fair hair over the tanned, thin face, with the pale blue eyes, the cheerful smile, a slender figure, and a quick, easy step."[240]

Emmy Eisenberg never got to climb with Paul that October. She had waited for him, in a way, since they first met, in his carefree university days, when he had discovered his destiny as a climber. Emmy followed Paul into the arms of the Evangelical church on November 20, 1913, a month after his funeral. On December 20, she married Hartwich, who was now a psychiatrist.

Tita had never taken the deaths of his friends and loved ones in his stride. He had risked his life to claim a memorial for his friend Ugo De Amicis's father and absented himself from the final discussion of the Piton Controversy to grieve for his wife, Marietta. Although he had other, more financially trying losses, Paul's death almost overwhelmed him. He had lost his battle with the Leipzig Section to stay on as custodian of the Vajolet hut after Maria died, and had bought his own land nearby on the Porta Neigre to build his own hut, in full view of the Vajolet Towers, Punta Emma and so many of the other climbs he and Paul had shared. In a gesture worthy of a medieval saint, he carried the stones for the hut with his hands and named it after his fallen Paolo. The Preuss hut still stands.

The German and Austrian alpine press was deeply shaken, if less emotional. The *German Alpine Times* published a full list of the climbs of its great correspondent, as well as his academic achievements, and the Alpine Club sections to which he belonged, in the Fraktur script in which his first manifesto had been published.[241] Testimonials poured in to the many Alpine Club sections of which Paul had been a member. The editor of the Alpen-Klub *Hoch Glück* yearbook represented the widespread need not just to mourn Paul's death but to derive some inspiration from his example: "The inexorable peak has snatched away one of our finest members. Although the wound burns, even this hard blow could not shake us from our position. All of us strive to reach the righteous heights… It is true that we have a seen a decrease in the number of climbs, but this is partly a consequence of the increase in [military] conscription of our members… Mountain climbing must always remain our main task… We must strive towards the heights."[242]

Geoffrey Winthrop Young was more circumspect: "Solitary climbing will always have its critics as well as its devotees. But with the feeling of regret for the premature death of a great climber and a fine personality comes also the feeling of pride that there are still men of the highest intellect in our generation who, with the full knowledge of all the easier and more profitable alternatives that life has to offer, continue to match their skill as it increases against increasing difficulty, and accept the issue with calm courage."[243]

Eulogists and bards of glorious death were soon to be in great demand. On the day Paul died, the empire of Austria-Hungary responded to an affront in Balkan politics by increasing the size of its army to two million. Just nine months later, Austria-Hungary began the First World War, which was to claim the lives of many of Paul's companions. Standards for conscription were low in Austria.

Paul, who had been rejected as unfit in peacetime, would have been drafted even if he had not volunteered.

Young German writer Ernst Jünger might have written about the crowds of young people pouring into the Stripsenjochhaus on weekends and roping up below the walls of the Eastern Alps in the first decades of the century when he said: "We had come from lecture halls, school desks and factory workbenches, and over brief weeks of training, we had bonded together into one large and enthusiastic group. Grown up in an age of security, we shared a yearning for danger, for the experience of the extraordinary." Sadly, however, he was describing the youngsters who enlisted in the German army in the autumn of 1914, and thus he concluded on a different note: "Surely the war would supply us with what we wanted; the great, the overwhelming, the hallowed experience... Anything to participate, anything not to stay at home!"[244]

Hans Dülfer volunteered because he believed that his contribution would end the war sooner. On June 13, 1915, he was in the trenches in France and made this note in his diary: "The anniversary of the Fleischbank East Wall is the day after tomorrow. I smoke my pipe in celebration."[245] Dülfer's father wrote to the Alpine Club Bayerland Section that on June 15, the anniversary of his Fleischbank climb, Hans had "held his post in the sharpest artillery fire, until a piece of shrapnel hit him in the neck."[246] Hanne Franz volunteered as a nurse and received the news of her lover's death in a field hospital on the Galician Front. She later married a Hungarian army captain and never climbed again.

Paul Jacobi was killed when his torpedo boat hit a British mine in the North Sea in 1915. Freud, Hartwich and Herzog survived the Western Front. Geoffrey Winthrop Young, although a conscientious objector, was decorated for his work in the Friends' Ambulance Unit and lost a leg in an artillery barrage. He continued to climb with a prosthesis after the war.

On May 23, 1915, Italy declared war against Austria-Hungary, in part to fulfill the irredentist dream of annexing the Welschtirol. The front line cut Tita Piaz's Fassa valley in half. Nieberl, Fiechtl, Hartwich and Schmidkunz all served on the Alpine Front and survived. There, Schmidkunz met Luis Trenker, the climber and filmmaker who became a pioneer of the *Bergfilm*. After the war, Schmidkunz ghost-wrote several of Trenker's books.

The alpine war left two million casualties and was a cultural and environmental disaster. Ancient villages were razed, huts were destroyed or vandalized, forests were cut down for firewood or fortifications. Valleys were shelled or inundated with poison gas; summits were used as gun emplacements and in some cases blown to bits. In November 1918, the Austrian army, facing defeat on its other fronts, ceded its ethnically Italian territories, and the rest of Austria-Hungary was divided into independent nations.

In the interwar period, climbers who had seen the Alps blown up with artillery and criss-crossed with military via ferratas no longer saw pitons used in any quantity as a serious threat to the integrity of the mountains. In 1933, Italian rock climbing master Emilio Comici roped up with Angelo and Giuseppe Dimai for the first ascent North Face of the Cima Grande. They used 150 metres of rope, 40 carabiners and 80 pitons. Things had changed since a dozen pitons placed in a climber's entire lifetime made them a notorious piton user. Comici was criticized by some, but the dam had broken.

The Italianization of the Dolomites could not have come a moment too soon for irredentists like Tita Piaz. His anarchist politics got him sent to a penal battalion on the Russian Front. Never one to keep his views to himself, he was imprisoned twice during the Italian fascist era and for nine months in 1944 by the Nazis. In 1949, his memoir, *A tu per tu con le crode*, was published. Tita was frank and revealing about Paul's risk taking. Mina told him that if Paul had taken Tita's advice and climbed with a greater concern for his own safety, he would still have been alive.[247] After the Second World War, Tita became the mayor of Pera di Fassa. He died in 1948 after a bicycle crash.

Günther von Saar spent a year and a half on the Russian Front, where he performed 800 operations. He also survived the Alpine Front, where he was a combat doctor. He died in Vienna in late 1918 in the influenza epidemic that killed 18,500 Austrians.

Lina Lauchheim spent the rest of her life in Altaussee, where she carefully tended her son's grave and, when she died in 1930, she was buried beside Paul, the last of her children to remain in Altaussee.

In 1938, the Nazis annexed Austria, forcing many people into excruciating choices. Walter Schmidkunz, a Jew, managed to survive the Holocaust by writing propaganda broadsheets for soldiers. After the war, he spent a year in prison for aiding the Nazis. Martin and Anna Freud fled to London with their family. Martin served in the British army and then became a tobacconist. Anna continued her father's psychoanalytical work. Neither climbed again. Paul's childhood friend Franz Mittler and college pal Walter Bing moved to America and became doctors. Sophie, who had married in the 1920s, fled with her husband when the Nazis confiscated their property. They moved to Los Angeles, where she died in 1959. Paul and Mina Relly moved to London. Mina died there in 1954, Paul Relly in the 1970s.

Alexander Hartwich, meanwhile, stayed in Vienna during the Nazi period. Saxon rock specialist Rudolf Fehrmann became an ardent Nazi; he died in Soviet captivity in 1948. Eduard Pichl, whose route on the Planspitze was Paul's first notable solo climb, was one of many famous Austrian climbers who supported Nazism.

Anti-Semitism threatened Paul's legacy. In 1927, Pichl wrote *Wiens Bergsteigertum*, a history of Viennese climbing, with no reference to Paul whatsoever. When Pichl was criticized for this omission by Josef Braunstein, the editor of the newsletter of the predominantly Jewish Donauland Section of the Alpine Club, he answered that he'd had no idea that Paul Preuss was from Vienna. It was an ominous prelude. Jews were eventually completely excluded from the Alpine Club, its properties and its trails. Although Messner has speculated on how Paul might have participated in the interwar Himalayan expeditions, the Nazification of these climbs precluded the participation of Jews. A racialized, nationalistic vision of alpinism took hold, in which the end justified the means, whether it be the deaths of Sherpas or the unlimited use of pitons or even aircraft. Throughout these dark years, the cosmopolitan Jew from Altaussee who eschewed even abseiling was all but forgotten.

Emmy Eisenberg, who declared Paul "her greatest love," proved it more than 30 years after his death, when she became the catalyst for the revival of his reputation.

After the funeral, she was given his diary and a piton hammer, the former much used and the latter hardly at all, and some other correspondence. She and Alexander Hartwich divorced after the First World War, and subsequently she befriended Italian rock climbing star Emilio Comici, 13 years her junior. In a photograph with Comici, she leans on a cane, presumably because of the knee that kept her from climbing with Paul in that summer of 1913. Comici, an admirer of fascist leader Benito Mussolini and in constant demand as an instructor and demonstrator of the virtues of the heroic Italian man, would die in 1940 in an abseiling accident. That same year, Emmy moved to Provence; there, under the Vichy government and then the Italian occupation, her being Jewish was slightly less of a liability than it had been in Austria. In the twenties, she married Otto Brioschi, a member of a wealthy Viennese family, and assumed the last name Hartwich-Brioschi.

Comici, meanwhile, had introduced Emmy to Italian alpine writer and filmmaker Severino Casara. She co-operated with him on his detailed hagiography *Preuss, l'alpinista leggendario* (Preuss, the Legendary Alpinist). Casara was very possessive of the numerous pieces of correspondence, route books and other records Emmy shared with him, and many of these items disappeared after 1951, when Casara finished writing his book, further obscuring the record of Paul's achievements.[248] Casara's manuscript was dedicated to Emmy and contained a whole chapter – and many other, not entirely relevant sections – praising her. "I've never met a woman so rich in charm and personality," he wrote, "and so simple and so human... Emmy is a timeless citizen of the world. She has Viennese charm, Italian emotions and a Parisian spirit, English calm and an Iberian veil of romance."[249] Emmy's correspondence, however, indicates that the admiration was less than mutual and that she was only co-operating with Casara to revive her lover's reputation.

Casara accepted her view, developed during four decades of

reflection, of Paul as a man whose death was foreshadowed in everything from his birth to his choice of climbs, as a sort of pre-ordained victim with foreknowledge of his own death. She may have developed this outlook in order to come to terms with her losses. Many climbers came to similar beliefs in hindsight, perhaps to justify the risks they continued to take, or out of a basic need for a hero. In 1976, Paul's friend Hermann Jaeger recounted a conversation in which Paul claimed that "I know that my hard solo climbing is only possible by sacrificing my life. I do not fear death in the mountains. When I meet my death, that is my destiny."[250]

Paul never quite advised climbers to put themselves at risk of death, however, unless they could climb with total security. When he spoke about paying the price of his climbing philosophies and making sacrifices, he meant sacrificing the climbs that he might achieve by compromising his personal code of climbing style, not losing his life.

In the 1970s, when Emmy was in her 90s, fate offered her one last, great opportunity to tell Paul's story.

Reinhold Messner rose to international fame in 1978, when he and Austrian Peter Habeler climbed Mount Everest without bottled oxygen. The same year, he became the first man to solo an 8000-metre peak with his ascent of Nanga Parbat. Messner was a vocal champion of fair and environmentally sustainable approaches to climbing. Famously, he accused climbers who packed expansion bolts of "carrying their courage in their rucksack." Bolts were not introduced to the Eastern Alps until the mid-1940s, but it is hard not to imagine Paul sharing Messner's views on them, had he lived to see one placed in his beloved limestone mountains.

Emmy saw a newspaper article about Messner that convinced her that he and Paul would have been kindred spirits. She sent him Paul's piton hammer and some of Paul's pitons, with the proviso that he keep them and pass them on to another, like-minded climber when he died. Given how much Paul despised pitons, it was an unusual legacy.

"I had the hammer in my cellar," said Messner, "and always when I saw it, I was thinking, 'Oh, I have to begin a museum.' Around this hammer, the whole museum idea began to grow."[251]

He eventually founded not one but a whole series of alpine museums. His museum on top of the Kronplatz was designed by British architect Zaha Hadid and is dedicated to traditional alpinism. Since it opened in 2015, Paul's hammer has been displayed there.

Emmy died in 1980. In 1986, on the centennial of Paul's birth, Messner published the first book about Paul in his native language, *Freiklettern mit Paul Preuss* (freeclimbing with Paul Preuss). He followed it in 1996 with *Der Philosoph des Freikletterns: Die Geschichte von Paul Preuss* (philosopher of free climbing: the story of Paul Preuss). Messner showed that Paul and his achievements should be understood as part of a wider context of culture and climbing in Europe at the turn of the century. He concluded that Paul might have become less of an outlier and attracted more climbers to his cause of pure climbing if he had not died so young.[252]

It is also possible, however, that Paul's philosophies would have changed. Many climbers change their interests and ethics over a long career. During Paul's short life, he shifted his positions at least a little about mountain guides and whether his approach was a personal vocation or one which all climbers should try to follow. He could perhaps have continued to evolve. We will never know.

German climbing historian Nicholas Mailänder sees Paul's contribution as part of an Eastern Alps synergy that has to be evaluated as a whole:

> The explosive development of rock climbing standards between 1910 and the First World War was not due to the effort of a single ingenious individual... Rather, every one of the "big four" – Herzog, Preuss, Fiechtl and Dülfer – made his indispensable contribution to the quantum leap in performance, which had been unthinkable a few years before.... Herzog had the determination to see dozens of modern rock climbing routes through to completion, a goal much aided by his introduction of the karabiner for running belays. Fiechtl invented the modern piton designed to be used with the karabiner that allowed a whole new way of working with the rope on hard

rock.… Dülfer synthesized all the ideas and techniques of the day in beautiful stylish movement on climbs once thought of as impossible.[253]

The immediate successors of Herzog, Fiechtl and Dülfer included Comici, Welzenbach and their contemporaries. There wasn't a single climber who followed Paul's path with anything like his uncompromising standard. Paul's contribution, according to Mailänder, cannot be judged by its singularity: "Like no one else the Viennese embodied the ethical core of rock climbing. All those competing with him agreed with this advocate of stylistic purity, that the ultimate and deepest experience in climbing depended on forsaking artificial utensils."[254]

On the centennial of Paul's death, in 2013, Austrian sculptor Walter Angerer's cut-out silhouette of Paul was erected on the shore of the Aussee. Through the gaps in the sculpture, you can see the walls of the Totes Gebirge Paul loved so much. In his outstretched right hand, he holds the hammer Emmy gave Messner, and he stares at it a little ambivalently, as if he is contemplating throwing it away. The hammer is, of course, incongruous as a symbol of Paul's climbing, but it is deeply enmeshed in the controversies of Paul's life and his relationship with Emmy. Without it, Messner's revival of Paul's legacy might never have happened.

Another monument to Paul was erected by the Gosau cable car station in 2015. The abstract portrayal of Paul in sheet metal, climbing a transparent structure and looking towards the Gosaukamm, from which he fell, was designed by students from the Halstatt technical college. During the unveiling, a local official said it was in the spirit of the statue of Jacques Balmat, who made the first ascent of Mont Blanc, in Chamonix. The unspoken difference between the two climbers is that Balmat lived to point at his climb afterwards.

Each year, the International Paul Preuss Society awards the Paul Preuss Award to a climber whose life or climbs have embodied Paul's spirit. Messner was the first winner. Others include guide and climber Hanspeter Eisendle, Austrian traditional climber

Albert Precht and extreme alpinists Hansjörg Auer and Alexander Huber.

In 2015, The Ausseer festival was renamed the Paul Preuss Festival. Now, annually, in addition to traditional dancing and a beer hall, lectures are given on the meaning of Paul Preuss to climbers, history and Ausseerland. Paul has truly taken his place in the cultural life of the mountains he loved so much and is one of the most well-known and beloved Ausseers in history.

In climbing, however, his achievements are studied mainly by historians and specialists on climbing ethics, and his reputation remains, if not suspect, something to be treated with delicacy. This is partly to be blamed on the way that alpinists like Riccardo Cassin oversimplified, or erroneously reported on, Paul's viewpoints and style. Cassin said that Paul "boasted that he had never driven a piton into a rock, and impulsively climbed faces as soon as they appeared in his field of vision," and died "a victim of his own theories."[255] While there is some truth in Cassin's objections to Paul's acceptance of risk, Cassin had made him into something of a caricature. After all, Paul wrote openly about driving pitons into the Trisselwand and carefully chose and prepared for his objectives, however much risk he accepted in their pursuit.

"To Bolt or Not to Be" and "Recommendations on the Preservation of Natural Rock for Adventure Climbing" were published in 2000 and 2012 respectively by the mountaineering commission of the international mountaineering body, known by the French acronym UIAA. The authors addressed changes in climbing protection use in the Alps in particular, but sought to lay down universally relevant principles. Both papers decried what the authors saw as the overuse of bolts and fixed protection on alpine routes and called for their reduction. "Those with a sense of history will appreciate climbing a classic route only if it remains untouched by the bolt," said the authors, "not devalued for financial gain or dumbed down by those who could not meet the challenge taken on by courageous pioneers."[256]

The authors' list of courageous pioneers included Albert Mummery, who died in an avalanche on Nanga Parbat in 1895 with his Gurkha porters; Italian Riccardo Cassin, who lived a hundred years and died in bed; Italian extreme alpinist and soloist Walter Bonatti, who died of cancer in Rome at 81; Swiss alpinist André Roch; Max Niederman, a Swiss hard rock climber active in the 1960s and '70s; Reinhold Messner; and German big wall and sport climber and soloist Alexander Huber. It is an inspiring list, but Paul Preuss and Georg Winkler are absent History embraces most enthusiastically those who espouse purist doctrines of climbing and survive, or at least do not die while actively pursuing purity. Those who die in pursuit of pure style – whether soloing or taking some other risk in name of their ideals – remain sensitive subjects.

Alpine martyrs, however, were not always an embarrassment. Paul's ghost appeared to Tita on the North Face of the Catinaccio and threatened to curse him with unhappiness if he used a piton for aid. Tita, at once spiritual and practical, saw nothing wrong with arguing that the ghost should give him a break: after all, he was 50 years old and the climb was difficult. It is fitting that Tita have the last word in this account of the life and climbs of his beloved Paolo – after all, he understood him better than anyone else.

[Paul] was the supreme holocaust on the altar of the mountains that he so completely and ardently loved. The atrocities of fate are merciless. That night [when Piaz learned of Paul's death] I blasphemed once more against the climbers and I scolded God and his Mother for the pain I felt... [Paul] dominated the rock like no other, with ideals, chivalry and speed, on an unbelievable triumphal march up the most difficult climbs of the Alps... Now he is at peace in the Styrian mountains, where he took the first and last steps of his career. In the little Altaussee cemetery, he lies buried alongside his dream. Perhaps sometime, when the deity of the mountain has stirred the gloomy mists, the immense Walls and the unlikely spells into a mystery, Preuss will rise from his cold grave to the crumbling, unsolved problems of the Gosaukamm, and when the moon's dead light turns the Dolomite peaks into silver oceans, and when the creatures of the cosmos, the stars, have baptized all of creation with their unreal and superhuman light, perhaps Paolo Preuss will return to his old world, the abandoned cliffs, and fly up there to his beloved Dolomites, where, on a predetermined summit, perhaps the Campanile Basso of the Brenta, the great Olympians will be summoned to him: Winkler, Mummery, Zsigmondy, and, amidst these Gods of the mountains, divinized by the moonlight, this Titan will tell of the mighty fantasies of his youth, his great days, hard victories, the unrealized, devious possibilities still within him and his insane thirst for altitude.[257]

Tita dubbed Paul the Lord of the Abyss, but Paul eventually made a feast for the ravens in the dark abyss that Tita warned him against. The two poles of climbing, as of life, are *Fürchten und Lieben*, fear and love. It was a lesson Paul taught but did not fully learn. For that reason, we might still look upon him as a kind of necessary saint called to a way that few can follow, rather than a climber like others are climbers. The little boy blessed with a love of mountains that made him close to fearless, who partook of mountains untouched by device or stratagem, as if they were the food of immortality, grew up to be the climber who died alone in the snow, on the rocks of the Mandlkogel.

Acknowledgements

Although any failures in this work are my own, its best qualities would never have been possible without the help of several people. Scott Smart undertook much of the research and helped with translations from French and Italian. Brian McKenzie also helped with the Italian translations. Nicholas Mailänder and Reinhold Messner contributed important ideas that changed my thinking as the work evolved. Reinhold's work in print and in his museums is largely responsible for keeping Paul Preuss's memory alive today. Randolph Burks, through his translations of the Piton Controversy essays, opened up an important primary resource in climbing history to the English-speaking world. Reg Smart, Gerry Banning, Jon Popowich, Katie Ives and Brandon Pullan all helped by reading drafts or contributing thoughts as the work progressed. Peter Norman's careful editing vastly improved the manuscript. Without Don Gorman and Rocky Mountain Books' continued support for my writing, this book would never have come to be published. Finally, I thank Katrina Kilroy, who gave me a place to finish this work and begin new ones.

Selected Bibliography

Burks, Randolph, ed. *The Collection of Essays Generally Known as the Mauerhakenstreit, the "Piton Dispute."* Published online by editor. https://issuu.com/randisi/docs/mauerhakenstreit_complete_illustrated.

Casara, Severino, *Alpinismo eroico.* Milan: Hoepli, 1942.

Casara, Severino. *Preuss, l'alpinista leggendario.* Milan: Longanesi, 1971.

Freud, Martin. *Glory Reflected.* London: Angus and Robertson, 1957.

Honnold, Alex, and David Roberts. *Alone on the Wall.* New York: W.W. Norton, 2016.

Ittlinger, Josef. *Handbuch des Alpinismus.* Lepizig: Grethlein, 1913.

Keller, Tait. *Apostles of the Alps: Mountaineering and Nation Building in Germany and Austria, 1860–1939.* Chapel Hill: University of North Carolina Press, 2016.

Lammer, Eugen Guido. *Jungborn.* Munich: Bergverlag Rudolf Rother, 1929.

Mailänder, Nicholas. *Im Zeichen des Edelweiss: Die Geschichte Münchens als Bergsteigerstadt.* Munich: AS Verlag, 2011.

Messner, Reinhold. *Der Philosoph des Freikletterns: Die Geschichte von Paul Preuss.* Munich: Piper Verlag, 2011.

Nieberl, Franz. *Klettern im Fels.* Munich: Verlag der Deutschen Alpenzeitung, 1909.

Piaz, Giovanni "Tita." *Le diable des Dolomites.* Paris: Arthaud, 1963.

Rey, Guido. *Peaks and Precipices: Scrambles in the Dolomites and Savoy.* London: Dodd, Mead, 1914.

Ring, Jim. *How the English Made the Alps.* London: John Murray, 2000.

Schmitt, Fritz. *Hans Dülfer, Bersteiger, Markstein, Legende.* Munich: Bruckmann, 1985.

Schweighofer, Astrid. *Religiöse Sucher in der Moderne: Konversionen vom Judentum zum Protestantismus in Wien um 1900.* Berlin: De Gruyter, 2015.

Scott, Doug. *Big Wall Climbing.* Oxford: Oxford University Press, 1974.

Tanesini, Arturo. *Tita Piaz, il diavolo delle Dolomiti.* Milan: Edizione L'Eroica, 1941.

Winkler, Georg. *Empor!: Georg Winklers Tagebuch. In memoriam. Ein Reigen von Bergfahrten hervorragender Alpinisten von heute.* Erich König, ed. Leipzig: Grethlein, 1906.

Young, Geoffrey Winthrop. *Mountain Craft.* London: Methuen: 1920.

Zsigmondy, Emil. *Die Gefahren der Alpen: Praktische Winke für Bergsteiger.* Leipzig: Frohberg, 1885.

Notes

Except where noted, all translations are by the author.

1   A Young Lady of Alsace, *Lucie's Diary of the Siege of Strasbourg* (London: Smith, Elder, 1871), 39.

2   Severino Casara, *Preuss, l'alpinista leggendario* (Milan: Longanesi, 1971), 13.

3   Section debt incurred by building trails and huts was noted with a mixture of admiration and alarm by Bavarian government accountant Norbert Zwickh. See, for example, "Geschichte der Section 1869-99," in M. von Prielmeyer, ed., *Geschichte der Alpenvereinssection München, als Denkschrift nach dreissigjährigem Bestehen* (Munich: Munich Verlag der Alpenvereinssection München, 1900), 385–87.

4   Joseph Lux, "Die Alpen in der Kunst," *Deutsche Alpenzeitung* (cited hereafter as *DA*) 1910–11, 187.

5   H. Rehm, M. Leberle, eds., *Jahres-Bericht der Sektion "Bayerland" München des Deutschen und Österreichischen Alpenvereins*, 4 (1900), 9–10.

6   *Zeitschrift des Deutschen und Öesterreichischen Alpenvereins* (1874), 57–58.

7   Sophie Freud, *Living in the Shadow of the Freud Family* (Westport, CT: Praeger, 2007), 26.

8   Martin Achrainer, "Der unermüdliche Lausbub Paul Preuss, von Aussen gesehen," *Bergauf*, February 2013, 10.

9   Casara, *Preuss*, 28.

10 Ibid., 36.

11 Paul Preuss, "Die Trisselwand," *Steirische Alpenpost* 27, no. 48 (1911), 12, cited in Reinhold Messner, *Der Philosoph des Freikletterns: Die Geschichte von Paul Preuss* (Munich: Piper Verlag, 2011), 157.

12 Ronald Hayman, *Thomas Mann: A Biography* (New York: Scribner, 1995), 96.

13 Frank Wedekind, *Spring Awakening*, trans. Edward Bond (London: Methuen, 2012), 7.

14 Eugen Guido Lammer, *Jungborn* (Munich: Bergverlag Rudolf Rother, 1929), 109.

15 Preuss, "Gross-Litzner-Nordwand," (cited hereafter as "Gross-Litzner"), *Mitteilungen des Deutschen und Österreichischen Alpenvereins* (cited hereafter as *MDÖAV*) 38 (1912), cited in Messner, *Philosoph*, 122–25.

16 Thomas Mann, *Buddenbrooks: The Decline of a Family*, trans. John E. Woods (New York: Random House, 1994), 427.

17 Casara, *Preuss*, 39.

18 Preuss, "Damenkletterei," *DA* 1912, 10–13, cited in Messner, *Philosoph*, 85.

19 Georg Winkler, letter to Eugen Guido Lammer, April 22, 1888, cited in *Empor! Georg Winklers Tagebuch. In memoriam. Ein Reigen von Bergfahrten hervorragender Alpinisten von heute*, Erich König, ed. (Leipzig: Grethlein, 1906), 79.

20 Casara, *Preuss*, 38.

21 Ibid., 253.

22 Fritz Schmitt, "Paul Preuss – zum fünfzigsten Todestag," *Jahrbuch des Deutschen Alpenvereins*, 1963, 184.

23 Stefan Zweig, *The Collected Novellas of Stefan Zweig*, trans. Anthea Bell (London: Pushkin Press, 2018), 28.

24 Mark Twain, *A Tramp Abroad*. 1880. (New York: Random House, 2003), 18.

25 Ibid., 17.

26 Martin Freud, *Glory Reflected* (London: Angus and Robertson, 1957), 157.

27 Ibid., 158.

28 Ibid., 157.

29 Alan McNee, *The New Mountaineer in Late Victorian Britain: Materiality, Modernity and the Haptic Sublime*, (London: Palgrave, 2016), 64.

30 Franz Nieberl, *Klettern im Fels* (Munich: Verlag der Deutschen Alpenzeitung, 1909).

31 Kerwin Lee Klein, "A Vertical World: The Eastern Alps and Modern Mountaineering," *Journal of Historical Sociology* 24, no. 4 (December 2011), 534.

32 Preuss, "Künstliche Hilfsmittel auf Hochtouren," *DA* August 1911, 242–44, cited in Messner, *Philosophe*, 50.

33 Ibid., cited in Messner, *Philosoph*, 51.

34 Alexander Hartwich, "Paul Preuss. Berg und Ski," *Zeitschrift des Alpenvereins Donauland* 180 (1937), 3–7, cited in Kurt Maix, "Paul Preuss – der Spaziergänger zu den Wolken," *Jugend am Berg* 4 (1963), 117.

35 Anna L. Staudacher, *Jüdisch-protestantische Konvertiten in Wien, 1782-1914*, vol. 1 (Frankfurt: Peter Lang, 2004), 190.

36 Astrid Schweighofer, *Religiöse Sucher in der Moderne: Konversionen vom Judentum zum Protestantismus in Wien um 1900* (Berlin: De Gruyter, 2015), 393.

37 Peter Grimm, *Walter Schmidkunz: Ein Klassiker im Hintergrund* (Munich: Bruckmann, 2010), 51.

38 John Alexander Williams, *Turning to Nature in Germany: Hiking, Nudism, and Conservation, 1900-1940* (Stanford: Stanford University Press, 2007), 131.

39 Sophie Freud, *Freud Family*, 26.

40 Nieberl, *Klettern im Fels*, 27.

41 Ibid., 28.

42 Preuss, "Putzi als Skiläuferin," *DA* March 1913.

43 Preuss, "Damenkletterei," cited in Messner, *Philosoph*, 85.

44 Emmy Eisenberg, letter to Reinhold Messner, cited in Claire Walter, "Reinhold Messner: A Man and His Museums," *Dwell*, August 1, 2016. Also, "I was [Preuss's] girlfriend for many years": Emmy Hartwich-Brioschi (née Eisenberg), letter to Paul Hübel, August 8, 1951.

45 Claire Walter, "Reinhold Messner: A Man and His Museums," *Dwell*, August 1, 2016.

46 Preuss, "Damenkletterei," cited in Messner, *Philosoph*, 85.

47 Ibid.

48 Harry Muré, *Jeanne Immink: Die Frau, die in die Wolken stieg* (Innsbruck: Tyrolia, 2010).

49 Reinhold Messner, *Der Philosoph des Freikletterns: Die Geschichte von Paul Preuss* (Munich: Piper Verlag, 2011), 10.

50 Preuss, diary entry: Casara, *Preuss*, plate 114.

51 Preuss, "Schlussbetrachtungen zur Amateurfrage," *Der Winter* 7 (1912), 80–83, cited in Messner, *Philosoph*, 48.

52 R.L.G. Irving, *The Romance of Mountaineering* (London: J.M. Dent & Sons, 1936), cited in Jim Ring, *How the English Made the Alps* (London: John Murray, 2000), 107.

53 Casara, *Preuss*, 55.

54 Preuss, "Gross-Litzner," cited in Messner, *Philosoph*, 162.

55 Nieberl, *Klettern im Fels*, 19.

56 Twain, *Tramp Abroad*, 210.

57 In *Climbing Rock*, Nieberl devotes only a page and a half to the subject of ice and snow climbing, which he says he only mentions in passing because "we don't have to deal with ice technology here [in the limestone Alps]" (33). He didn't think enough was even known on the subject to warrant a book until he wrote *Das Gehen auf Eis und Schnee*.

58 Schweighofer, *Konversionen*, 324.

59 Tait Keller, *Apostles of the Alps: Mountaineering and Nation Building*

in Germany and Austria, 1860–1939 (Chapel Hill: University of North Carolina Press, 2016), 75.

60 Casara, *Preuss*, 55.

61 Martin Luther, *Der Kleine Katechismus* (1529), accessed October 29, 2018, http://www.bernhard-kaiser.homepage.t-online.de/downloads/ lutherldkatechismus.pdf.

62 *Martin Luther's Works*, vol. 12, *Liturgy and Prayer*, Jaroslav Pelikan, ed. (Philadelphia: Fortress Press), 107.

63 Preuss, "Eine Frühlingsfahrt in das Zillertal," *DA* 1913, cited in Messner, *Philosoph*, 203.

64 In 1880, British mountaineer Cecil Slingsby used skis to ascend a number of mountains in Norway, and is sometimes seen as the father of ski mountaineering, but his efforts were little known in the German-speaking world and not widely published until 1904.

65 Nieberl, *Klettern im Fels*, 25.

66 Since most of Paul Preuss's route book is missing, we cannot be sure that he did not begin to record his skiing experiences earlier.

67 Rudolf Schlesinger, *Central European Democracy and Its Background* (New York: Routledge, 1955), 6.

68 Preuss, "Jagd und Skitouristik," *DA* February 1913, 35, 40, cited in Messner, *Philosoph*, 112.

69 Ibid., cited in Messner, *Philosoph*, 113.

70 Ernst Enzensperger, "Alpenfahrten der Jugend: Nach einem Vortrag in der Alpenvereinssektion München," *MDÖAV* 39 (1913), 39–40.

71 Preuss, "Hunting," cited in Messner, *Philosoph*, 114.

72 Ibid.

73 Ibid.

74 Nieberl, *Klettern im Fels*, 25.

75 Eugen Oertel, "Der Frage des Schutzhütten in Winter auf der Hauptversammlung in Regensburg," *MDÖAV* 39 (1913), 225–28.

76 O. Reuther, "Unsere Schutzhütten in Winter: Ein Beitrag zur

Benutzungfrage," *MDÖAV* 39 (1913), 307–30, cited in Keller, *Apostles,* 75.

77 Preuss, "Das Winterhütten-Problem," *Der Winter* 5 (1911), 365–66, cited in Messner, *Philosoph,* 111–12.

78 Ibid.

79 Martin Freud, *Glory Reflected,* 157.

80 Sigmund Freud, letter to Karl Abraham, May 29, 1918, in *The Complete Correspondence of Sigmund Freud and Karl Abraham, 1907–1925,* Ernst Falzeder, ed. (London: Karnac, 2002), 378.

81 Martin Freud, *Glory Reflected,* 158.

82 Preuss [P. Schulze, pseud.], "Alpenvereinshütten in Winter," *MDÖAV* 38 (1912), 91–93.

83 Preuss, "Amateur," 80–83, cited in Messner, *Philosoph,* 48.

84 Ibid., cited in Messner, *Philosoph,* 49.

85 Leslie Stephen, *The Playground of Europe* (New York: G.P. Putnam, 1909), 267–68.

86 Arturo Tanesini, *Tita Piaz, il diavolo delle Dolomiti* (Milan: Edizione L'Eroica, 1941), 5.

87 Giovanni "Tita" Piaz, *Le diable des Dolomites* (Paris: Arthaud, 1963), 30.

88 Ibid., 45.

89 Piaz, *Le diable,* 39.

90 Klein, "Vertical World," 520.

91 Piaz, *Le diable,* 93. For more on the realities behind the Piaz myth, see Luciana Palla, *Tita Piaz a confronto con il suo mito* (Trento: Istitut Cultural Ladin, 2006).

92 Casara, *Preuss,* 81.

93 Keller, *Apostles,* 81.

94 Ben M. Anderson, "The Construction of an Alpine Landscape:

Building, Representing, and Affecting the Eastern Alps, c. 1885–1914," *Journal of Cultural Geography* 29, no. 2 (June 2012), 159.

95 *Sport-Ausstellungs-Zeitung & Tagesprogramm: Officielles Organ der Allgemeinen Deutschen Sportausstellung München 1899* 32, no. 3, cited in Anderson, "Construction," 159.

96 Karl Müller, "Das Alpine Museum zu München," *MDÖAV* 37 (1911), 15, cited in Anderson, "Construction," 164.

97 "Die Eröffnung des alpinen Museums zu München," *MDÖAV* 37 (1911), 292, cited in Anderson, "Construction," 164.

98 Nicholas Mailänder, *Im Zeichen des Edelweiss* (Munich: AS Verlag, 2006), 113.

99 "Aus den Ersten Jahren," *Berglands Chronik* (publication details unavailable), Deutscher Alpenverein archives, DAV PER 2 SG/94/0 Teil 1, accessed October 29, 2018, https://www.historisches-alpenarchiv.org/data/dokumente/main/32/00131338_m.pdf.

100 Preuss, letter to Sigmund Preuss, August 29, 1910: Casara, *Preuss,* plate 102.

101 Casara, *Preuss,* 51.

102 Günther Freiherr von Saar, "In Memoriam, Paul Preuss," *The Alpine Journal* 28, no. 203 (February 1914), 2.

103 Adolf Mokrejs, "'…wie ein Vogel fliegt': Zum hundertsten Geburtstag von Paul Preuss," *Mitteilungen des Deutschen Alpenverein,* June 1986, 63.

104 Karl Abraham, "Giovanni Segantini, ein psycho-analytischer Versuch," *Schriften zur angewandten Seelenkunde* 11 (1911), 54.

105 For more on Paul Rudolph Preuss, see Paul R. Preuss, *Expedition nach Central- und Südamerika: 1899/1900* (Berlin: Kolonial-Wirtschaftlichen Komitees, 1901); and Corey Ross, *Ecology and Power in the Age of Empire: Europe and the Transformation of the Tropical World* (Oxford: Oxford University Press, 2017).

106 Klein, "Vertical World," 531.

107 Nieberl, *Klettern im Fels,* 41.

108 Guido Rey, *Peaks and Precipices: Scrambles in the Dolomites and Savoy* (London: Dodd, Mead, 1914), 117–18.

109 Preuss, "Die Nordkante des Grossen Ödsteins," *MDÖAV* 38 (1912), cited in Messner, *Philosoph*, 163.

110 Fritz Schmitt, *Hans Dülfer, Bersteiger, Markstein, Legende* (Munich: Bruckmann, 1985), 21.

111 Schmitt, *Hans Dülfer*, 21.

112 Nicholas Mailänder, "Die Ursprünge des Freikletterns," *BergSteigen* (2016), 148.

113 Casara, *Preuss*, 176.

114 Horst Höfler, "Tita Piaz – Legenden der Totenkirchl-Westwand," *Bergsteiger*, July 2009, accessed August 3, 2018, http://bergsteiger.de/ bergszene/reportagen/tita-piaz-legenden-der-totenkirchl-westwand.

115 Rey, *Peaks and Precipices*, 129–30, cited in Klein, "Vertical World," 538.

116 The upper half of the ridge was completed in 1924 by J. Ostler.

117 Casara, *Preuss*, 187.

118 Nieberl, *Klettern im Fels*, 19.

119 *Pubblicazione commemorativa della Società degli alpinisti tridentini nel suo cinquantenario (1872–1922)* (Trento: Società degli Alpinisti Tridentini, 1922), 60. Hans Barth reported on the third ascent in *Zeitschrift des Deutschen und Österreichischen Alpenvereins* (1907), 335, but seemed unaware of this flag. There were, however, other flag incidents, like the one on Cima Brenta in 1912.

120 Casara, *Preuss*, 190.

121 Ibid., 184.

122 Preuss, "Guglia di Brenta, Neuer Gipfelstieg durch die Ostwand," *MDÖAV* 37 (1911), 274, cited in Messner, *Philosoph*, 138.

123 Casara, *Preuss*, 190.

124 Ibid., 206.

125 Ibid., 203.

126 Preuss, "Die Trisselwand," cited in Messner, *Philosoph*, 156.

127 Preuss, "Damenkletterei," cited in Messner, *Philosoph*, 90–91.

128 Monika Estermann, Ursula Rautenberg, eds., *Archiv für Geschichte des Buchwesens*, vol. 64 (Berlin: De Gruyter, 2009), 182.

129 Keller, 53.

130 Helge Marguerite Heinrich, *Die 'Münchner Lesebogen' und ihr Herausgeber Walter Schmidkunz* (Munich: Literatur in Bayern, 2009), 1.

131 Preuss, "Künstliche Hilfsmittel auf Hochtouren" (translated as "Artificial Aids on Alpine Routes" and cited henceforth as Preuss, "Artificial Aids"), *DA* 1911, 242, in *The Collection of Essays Generally Known as the Mauerhakenstreit, the "Piton Dispute*," ed. and trans. Randolph Burks, accessed October 28, 2018, https://issuu.com/randisi/docs/mauerhakenstreit_complete_illustrated (cited hereafter as Burks, *Piton Dispute*), 1. I have occasionally referenced the originals or made my own translations; notably, Burks translates *Skilaüferin* as snowshoeing, but I translate it as skiing.

132 Josef Ittlinger, *Handbuch des Alpinismus* (Lepizig: Grethlein, 1913), 21.

133 Preuss, "Artificial Aids," cited in Burks, *Piton Dispute*, 3.

134 Ibid., cited in Burks, *Piton Dispute*, 4.

135 Nieberl, *Klettern im Fels*, 40.

136 Preuss, "Artificial Aids," cited in Burks, *Piton Dispute*, 5.

137 Hans Dülfer, "Zusammenfassung, Künstliche Hilfsmittel auf Hochtouren" *MDÖAV* 38 (1912), 69–70, cited in Burks, *Piton Dispute*, 25.

138 Messner, *Philosoph*, 28–30.

139 Giovanni "Tita" Piaz, "Künstliche Hilfsmittel auf Hochtouren, Erwiderung" (translated as "Artificial Aids on Alpine Routes, a Response," and cited hereafter as Piaz, "Artificial Aids Response"), *DA* October 1911, cited in Burks, *Piton Dispute*, 6.

140 Ibid.

141 Ibid.

142 Ibid., cited in Burks, *Piton Dispute*, 7.

143 Ibid., cited in Burks, *Piton Dispute*, 6.

144 Ibid., cited in Burks, *Piton Dispute*, 7–8.

145 Ibid., cited in Burks, *Piton Dispute*, 8.

146 Preuss, "Entgegnung," *DA* October 1911, cited in Burks, *Piton Dispute*, 9.

147 Ibid., cited in Burks, *Piton Dispute*, 11.

148 Ibid., cited in Burks, *Piton Dispute*, 10.

149 Franz Nieberl, "Gewitter," *MDÖAV* 37 (1911), 265–67 (translated and cited hereafter as "Thunderstorm"), cited in Burks, *Piton Dispute*, 12.

150 The Seven Weeks' War with Prussia in 1866 had left thousands of Austrian casualties and cost the emperor Venetia. Revanchist elements of Austrian society were quick to point out that huts owned by German sections were opened with ceremonies where "Das Lied der Deutschen," with the refrain "Deutschland über alles," was sung. German section huts flew German flags, displayed pictures of the Prussian war minister, Bismarck, who masterminded the Seven Weeks' War, and in one tone-deaf episode, boasted a war memorial to pan-German politician Karl Hoffmann on the Grossglockner (Keller, *Apostles*, 54, 59). German clubs aspiring to build huts in the Italian-speaking Dolomites were also viewed with suspicion. The Società degli Alpinisti Tridentini won a long, drawn-out lawsuit against the German and Austrian Alpine Club for building the Bremer Hut in the Bocca di Brenta – a suit that almost bankrupted the sections involved.

151 Nieberl, "Thunderstorm," cited in Burks, *Piton Dispute*, 12. The Damascus Blood Libel Case of 1840, in which rabbis were accused of murdering a monk, fascinated the Christian West, and especially Austrians. The fact that the rabbis were found innocent did little to dispel the rumour that Jews, like Moloch, murdered innocent Christians.

152 Ibid., cited in Burks, *Piton Dispute*, 15.

153 Ibid.

154 For the Jew as bacillus in *fin de siècle* Europe, see Marvin Perry, *Western Civilization: A Brief History* (Boston: Wadsworth, 2009), 367.

155 Nieberl, "Thunderstorm," cited in Burks, *Piton Dispute*, 16.

156 Doug Scott, *Big Wall Climbing* (Oxford: Oxford University Press, 1974), 19.

157 Preuss, "Künstliche Hilfsmittel auf Hochtouren, Eine Entgegnung von Paul Preuss in Wien" (translated as "Artificial Aids on Alpine Climbs, a Reply from Vienna by Paul Preuss" and cited hereafter as "Vienna Reply"), *MDÖAV* 37 (1911), 282, cited in Burks, *Piton Dispute*, 18.

158 Ibid., cited in Burks, *Piton Dispute*, 18.

159 Ibid.

160 Ibid., cited in Burks, *Piton Dispute*, 12.

161 Ibid., cited in Burks, *Piton Dispute*, 19.

162 Ibid.

163 O. Jüngling, "Künstliche Hilfsmittel," *Bergheil-Kalender* (1912), cited in Preuss, "Vienna Reply," and Burks, *Pito Piton Dispute, n Dispute*, 20.

164 Messner, *Philosoph*, 219–21.

165 Preuss, "Vienna Reply," cited in Burks, *Piton Dispute*, 21.

166 Paul Jacobi, "Randglossen," *DA* November 1911, 99–100, cited in Burks, *Piton Dispute*, 2.

167 Ibid.

168 Ibid.

169 Piaz, "Artificial Aids Response," 174.

170 Preuss, "Künstliche Hilfsmittel auf Hochtouren, Erwiderung, Paul Jacobi," *DA* January 1912, 115–16, cited in Burks, *Piton Dispute*, 25.

171 Ibid.

172 Ibid., cited in Burks, *Piton Dispute*, 26.

173 Ibid., cited in Burks, *Piton Dispute*, 27.

174 Ibid.

175 Dülfer, "Summary."

176 Ibid., cited in Burks, *Piton Dispute,* 28

177 Oertel also invented the avalanche cord to help find skiers buried in avalanches.

178 Dülfer, "Summary," *MDÖAV* 38 (1912), cited in Burks, *Piton Dispute,* 29.

179 Ibid.

180 Ibid.

181 Ibid., cited in Burks, *Piton Dispute,* 30.

182 Ibid.

183 Ibid.

184 Keller, *Apostles,* 31.

185 Ibid., 32.

186 Casara, *Preuss,* preface.

187 Ibid.

188 The most comprehensive lecture topic list is in Casara, *Preuss,* 353.

189 Joseph Lux, "Artistic Secrets of the Kodak," reproduced in full in Mark Jarzombek, "Joseph August Lux: Theorizing Early Amateur Photography – In Search of a 'Catholic Something,'" *Centropa* 4.1 (January 2004), 85–86.

190 Preuss, "Ödsteins," cited in Messner, *Philosoph,* 163.

191 Preuss, "Guglia di Brenta," cited in Messner, *Philosoph,* 138.

192 Preuss, "Gross–Litzner," cited in Messner, *Philosoph,* 126.

193 Preuss, "Trafoier Eiswand (Nordwand) Bäckmanngrat," *DA* 1912, 165–69, cited in Messner, *Philosoph,* 130.

194 Preuss, "Ödsteins," cited in Messner, *Philosoph,* 162.

195 Keller, *Apostles,* 19.

196 Preuss, "Das Kaiserdenkmal," *DA* 1913, 37–40, cited in Messner, *Philosoph,* 109.

197 Preuss, "Hunting," cited in Messner, *Philosoph,* 113.

198 Preuss, "Zillertal," cited in Messner, *Philosoph*, 203.

199 Preuss, "Eine Überschreitung des Steinernen Meeres," *DA* February 13, 1913, cited in Messner, *Philosoph*, 176.

200 Schmitt, *Hans Dülfer*, 284.

201 Casara, *Preuss*, 267.

202 Geoffrey Winthrop Young, *On High Hills: Memories of the Alps* (1924), quoted in Jim Ring, *How the English Made the Alps* (London: John Murray, 2000), 41.

203 Oscar Eckenstein, "Über Steigeisentechnik," *Sterreichische Alpenzeitung* 30, no. 764 (June 1908).

204 Geoffrey Winthrop Young, *Mountain Craft* (London: Methuen, 1920), 138.

205 Ibid., 139.

206 Preuss, "Zum Unglück in der Montblanc-Gruppe," cited in Messner, *Philosoph*, 34.

207 Alan Lyall, "The Matterhorn Lithographs of 1865," *The Alpine Journal* 100 (1995), 215.

208 Ibid., 216.

209 Hermann Jaeger, letter to the Deutscher Alpenverein, January 28, 1976.

210 Preuss, letter to Aldo Bonacossa, August 23, 1912: Casara, *Preuss*, plate 108.

211 Casara, *Preuss*, 252.

212 Ibid., 254.

213 Fries was a movie actor, but Piaz exaggerates her status as a climber. Elsewhere he commented he had brought her along to play to Paul's fondness for female company.

214 Piaz, *Le diable*, 169.

215 Preuss, "Gross-Litzner," Messner, *Philosoph*, 123.

216 Piaz, *Le diable*, 170.

217 Ugo di Vallepiana, "Paul Preuss, Halbjude und 'a lustiger Bua,'" *Alpinismus* 11, no. 3 (1973), 28. French King Henry IV said, "Paris is worth a mass," when he converted to Catholicism in 1593 in order to keep the throne.

218 Preuss, postcard to Lina Preuss, August 12, 1913: Casara, *Preuss,* plate 109.

219 Casara, *Preuss,* 268.

220 Wibke Backhaus, *Bergkameraden, Soziale Nahbeziehungen im alpinistischen Diskurs (1860–2010)* (Frankurt: Kampus Verlag, 2016).

221 Preuss, postcard to Lina Preuss, August 12, 1913: Casara, *Preuss,* plate 109.

222 Casara, *Preuss,* 269.

223 Saar, "In Memoriam," 4.

224 Preuss, letter to Lina Preuss, August 29, 1913: Casara, *Preuss,* plate 111.

225 Preuss, letter to Emmy Eisenberg, September 10, 1913: Casara, *Preuss,* plate 112.

226 Saar, "In Memoriam," 1.

227 Casara, *Preuss,* 275.

228 Ibid., 281.

229 Ibid., 267.

230 For an account of objects found near the site of Preuss's death, see Willi von End, "Grosser Manndlkogel: Seine Ersteigungsgeschichte," *Österreichische Alpenzeitung,* July 1972, 90–97.

231 A short list of expert climbers who have died climbing solo includes Georg Winkler, Jimmy Jewell, Derek Hersey, Jimmy Ray Forrester, John Bachar, Akihira Tawara, Michael Ybarra, Vik Hendrickson, Robert Steele, Dwight Bishop, Tony Wilmott, John Taylor, Bugs McKeith, and John Lauchlan.

232 Alex Honnold and David Roberts, *Alone on the Wall* (New York: W.W. Norton, 2016), 195.

233 End, "Grosser Manndlkogel," 94.

234 "Hoch Glück," 8.

235 End, "Grosser Manndlkogel," 93.

236 Kurt Schall and Thomas Jekel, *Dachsteingebirge und Gosaukamm: Die 250 schönsten Kletterrouten, Klettersteige und Schirouten* (Alland: Schall-Verlag, 1996), cited in Tenreiter Clemens, "Nördlicher Mandlkogel 2251 m, Nordkante," accessed October 5, 2018, http://www.lawine.salzburg.at/tour/index2.php?id=14386.

237 Casara, *Preuss*, 282.

238 *Jahres-Bericht des Alpen-Klub Hoch Glück 1912/13* 7 (1914) (cited hereafter as *Hoch Glück*), 8

239 Saar, "In Memoriam," 8.

240 Alexander Hartwich, "Paul Preuss, Blätter der Erinnerung," *Berg und Ski, Zeitschrift des Alpenvereins Donauland* 17, no. 180 (January 1937), 3–7, cited in Messner, *Philosoph*, 255.

241 Each section had different requirements for membership, some taking only educated men, others emphasizing climbing records of different kinds, still others admitting only skiers, so being a member of many sections proved that you were a well-rounded alpinist.

242 *Hoch Glück*, 9.

243 Geoffrey Winthrop Young, "The Fatal Accident of Dr. Paul Preuss," *Alpine Journal* 27, no. 202 (1913), 429.

244 Ernst Jünger, *Storm of Steel* (London: Penguin, 2004), 5.

245 Schmitt, *Hans Dülfer*, 50.

246 Ibid., 50.

247 Piaz, *Le diable*, 150.

248 Casara, *L'Arte di arrampicare di Emilio Comici* (Milan: Hoepli, 1957), 70.

249 Casara, *Preuss*, 41.

250 Jaeger, letter to Deutscher Alpenverein.

251 Richard Whistler, "Reinhold Messner: King of the mountains," *Financial Times*, August 7, 2015, accessed August 8, 2018, https://www.ft.com/content/ecf0ef20-3a8c-11e5-bbd1-b37bc06f590c.

252 Messner, *Philosoph*, 220.

253 Mailänder, *Im Zeichen*, 113.

254 Ibid.

255 Riccardo Cassin, "Italian Climbing Between the Wars," trans. S.K. Armistead, *Alpine Journal 77* (1972).

256 *UIAA Recommendations on the Preservation of Natural Rock for Adventure Climbing* (Bern: International Mountaineering And Climbing Federation, 2012), 6, accessed August 8, 2018, https://www.theuiaa.org/documents/declarations/13-01-2014-revision-The-Preservation-of-Natural-Rock-for-Adventure-Climbing.pdf.

257 Piaz, *Le diable*, cited in Casara, *Preuss*, 286–87.

Index

244